ONE DAY AT A TIME

365 Innovations, Discoveries, and Triumphs in World History

BRUCE WILSON, JR.

CONTENTS

I dedicate this book to my wonderful family and friends who have added so much joy and purpose to my life. I especially want to express gratitude to my dear parents, Carolyn and Bruce Wilson, my ever diligent and mindful sister Allison, and my beloved brother Lance.

INTRODUCTION

What did Robert the Bruce learn from a spider? Why did Botticelli throw his paintings into a bonfire? How did the ancient Chinese use bones to predict the future?

In the five thousand years of written records, history has left behind many puzzles and mysteries. These stories don't usually make it into the history curriculum, even though they provide a window into the past.

Too many history books focus on wars and plagues, battles and assassinations.

But what about the positive moments in history?

The past five thousand years have seen stunning human discoveries about the world around us. Travelers brought back tales of distant lands that seemed like fiction, rulers triumphed with the odds against them, and builders created monuments that stood for centuries or millennia.

Many of these moments don't make it into the history books.

The best-seller list includes books about World War II, great presidents, and not-so-great presidents. Most history books focus on the 20th century, leaving out thousands of years before the modern era. By only looking at the recent past, we lose the humbling scale of history.

And then there's the strange side of history—the dancing plagues and frost fairs—that gets cut from textbooks focused on dates and great men.

But the strangest stories in history tell us more about the past than memorizing the presidents in chronological order.

Picture London in 1814. King George III rules over the United Kingdom—though not the American colonies. British troops march on Washington, D.C., where they set the White House on fire. And in London, cold temperatures turn the River Thames into solid ice.

That year, London held a frost fair on the frozen river. Stalls sold hot pies and spiced cider to visitors. Londoners danced on the ice to enchanting music. And when the ice melted, the frost fairs ended.

Or imagine life in 10th century China, where the women in the imperial harem filled their time by inventing a new game: playing cards. Thanks to China's advances in printing and papermaking, "the game of leaves" soon became popular across Asia.

When playing cards reached Europe in the 14th century, the suits evolved from the Chinese suit of coins to swords, cups, staves, and coins.

Then sail to India in 1497 alongside Vasco da Gama. The first European to sail to Asia, da Gama thought he would impress the royal court in Calicut with his gifts.

But when the Portuguese explorer pulled out cloth, honey, hats, and oil, the king's advisors laughed. Even the poorest merchant from Mecca brought gold to the king. Da Gama and other European travelers soon realized their idea of luxury didn't measure up with the riches of the East.

One Day at a Time takes you through 365 moments in human history, from the development of writing through the 21st century.

These windows into history capture the evolution of technology, the increasing connections between distant lands, and the individual triumphs that make history so fascinating.

Learn how a female detective went undercover as Abraham Lincoln's sister to save the president from assassination in the early years of the Civil War.

Hear the story of the first human blood transfusion—and why scientists transfused animal blood into their human subjects.

Visit London's first coffee house and find out why some condemned the "newfangled, abominable, heathenish liquor called coffee."

Puzzle over the dancing plague in Strasbourg, where compulsive dancing killed Germans who claimed they couldn't stop.

In the 21st century, it's easy to spend more time thinking about where we'll go next rather than where we've been. New discoveries, new technologies, and new challenges seem right around the corner. But we can only understand the present—and the future—by knowing where we've been.

By looking back at five thousand years of history in 365 snapshots, *One Day at a Time* captures the human imagination and our ability to flourish and grow as a species. If we don't understand the past, we can't meet the future.

That's one goal of *One Day at a Time*: to invite everyone to learn more about history, one day a time, in a writing style that is succinct, compelling, and relevant to our modern experience. We now live in a "high tech, low touch" world—with both positive and negative consequences. All of us can benefit from considering the "collective wisdom of the ages" portrayed in the 365 historical events covered here.

As we travel through thousands of years of history, meeting people from different times and places, we should always remember the common humanity that unites us all.

History began with the development of writing—everything before that monumental leap belongs to prehistory. So that's where we'll start. In the Fertile Crescent, where the first cities arose nearly 10,000 years ago, ancient Sumerians needed a way to record economic transactions. The first marks pressed into dry clay gave birth to history.

THE BIRTH OF HISTORY (3100 BCE-1000 BCE)

C. 3100 BCE: THE FIRST KNOWN WRITING SYSTEM EMERGES IN SUMER.

In ancient Sumer, a scribe pressed his stylus into wet clay, leaving behind a wedge-shaped mark. With a few scratches, the scribe created the first known writing system—cuneiform script. Before 3100 BCE, Sumerian scribes pressed dots into clay to represent different goods and commodities. A token might record jars of oil or heads of sheep.

Cuneiform unlocked thousands of possibilities. Writing soon went far beyond recording economic transactions. Within centuries, scribes began pressing stories into clay. In the ancient cities of Sumer, kings recorded their deeds on the walls of their palaces, creating records that would last for nearly 5,000 years. One small step—the development of writing—ushered in a new era of history.

C. 3000 BCE: THE EGYPTIANS DEVELOP A HIEROGLYPHIC SCRIPT AND CREATE PAPYRUS.

Five thousand years ago the Egyptian god Thoth handed down writing to the people of the Nile River Valley—or, at least, that's what the ancient Egyptians claimed. They called their script *medu-netjer*, or "the god's words," and today we call them hieroglyphs.

Scribes chiseled hieroglyphs into the walls of tombs and brushed ink on papyrus, a paper created from reeds. The nearby Sumerians recorded economic transactions with their script, but in Egypt, writing connected the living with powerful forces—Egyptians believed that writing could transform reality itself and link man with divine powers. By 1550 BCE, Egyptian mummies carried *The Book of the Dead* into the afterlife, where powerful spells protected their soul on its long and dangerous journey.

C. 3000 BCE: EGYPTIANS PLAY THE WORLD'S FIRST KNOWN BOARD GAME, SENET.

Board games are nearly as old as written history itself. Around 3000 BCE, Egyptians were already playing the world's first known board game, called senet. In the game, players faced each other on opposite sides of a gameboard, moving their pawns on a grid of 30 squares. Senet quickly spread to nearby civilizations and people in the Near East played it for thousands of years.

No one knows the exact rules of senet. Paintings show the Egyptian queen Nefertiti playing senet, and snippets of text indicate that players relied on strategy and luck to win. While senet's rules remain mysterious, the game's popularity for millennia shows how much people love board games.

C. 2850 BCE: THE CHINESE BEGIN UNWINDING THE COCOON OF SILKWORMS TO SPIN IT INTO SILK.

One day the Empress Leizu sat in her garden drinking tea. With a splash, a silkworm cocoon fell into her cup, surprising the young woman. Reaching into the tea, Leizu began to unroll the cocoon, surprised to find thread she could weave. Empress Leizu thus became the first to create silk, according to Confucius.

By 2850 BCE, the Chinese had mastered silk. Soon, the fine fabric became one of China's most valuable exports, and rivals tried to unravel the secret of silk production. In ancient Rome, impressed customers assumed the fabric somehow came from tree leaves. The baffled Romans named China *Seres*, or silk people.

C. 2800 BCE: THE EGYPTIANS INTRODUCE THE 365-DAY CALENDAR.

The Sumerians counted time by the moon, dividing the year into lunar months. When the calendar strayed too far from the solar year, Sumerians simply threw in a leap month. Nearby Egypt took a different approach, and by around 2800 BCE the Egyptians were using a solar calendar with 365 days—the same type of calendar still used today.

Egyptians divided the year into three seasons that lasted 120 days each. Each season contained four 30-day months. At the end of the 360 day calendar, Egyptians added five days between years. On these days, Egyptians celebrated the birthdays of their gods. The Romans later adapted the Egyptian calendar, making it a direct predecessor of today's calendars.

C. 2560 BCE: IN EGYPT, CONSTRUCTION OF THE GREAT PYRAMID OF GIZA IS COMPLETED.

Egyptians placed the final stone on the Great Pyramid of Giza while wooly mammoths still walked the earth. Built as a tomb for an Egyptian pharaoh, the massive structure contains over two million blocks of granite and limestone. Someone standing before the pyramid in 2560 BCE would have seen a dazzling white structure since the Egyptians encased the pyramid in polished limestone.

The monumental building project took decades and put tens of thousands of Egyptians to work. But slaves didn't build the pyramids— pharaohs hired and paid Egyptians to construct the tomb. For nearly four centuries, the Great Pyramid stood as the tallest man-made structure.

C. 2500 BCE: THE LARGEST STONES ARE PUT INTO PLACE AT STONEHENGE.

In Briton, Neolithic builders raised massive stones at Stonehenge around the year 2500 BCE. But where did they find the stones, and how did they create the massive monument centuries before the wheel reached the British Isles? The builders carried stones weighing several tons found 200 miles away in Wales.

Stonehenge has baffled visitors for centuries. A 17th-century duke dug into the ground at the center of the monument, certain he would find treasure. But Stonehenge was almost certainly a religious burial site, not the world's largest treasure chest. Still, the mystery of Stonehenge continues to entrance visitors today.

C. 2150–2030 BCE: THE EPIC OF GILGAMESH IS WRITTEN DOWN FOR THE FIRST TIME.

In the Sumerian city of Uruk, Gilgamesh ruled as king. He built mighty walls and led men to victory in battle. But Gilgamesh thought only of his own glory—until he set off on a quest to understand the meaning of life. After failing in his search for immortality, Gilgamesh realizes that death is inevitable. Instead of chasing glory, he devotes himself to building a legacy that will live beyond his death.

In history's first epic poem, Sumerians wrestled with what gives life meaning and what happens after death. For over 4,000 years, the Epic of Gilgamesh has reminded readers to focus not on immediate rewards but on the larger question of what it means to be human.

C. 1754 BCE: THE CODE OF HAMMURABI LISTS BABYLONIAN LAWS.

An eye for an eye, a tooth for a tooth. The powerful Babylonian king Hammurabi chiseled his code of laws into a massive black pillar that stands over seven feet tall. His laws laid down the punishments for dozens of crimes, demanding retribution for harm. Atop the list of rules stands a carving of Hammurabi himself, receiving the law from Babylonia's god of justice.

While the punishments in the Code of Hammurabi could be severe—cheating carried a sentence of being thrown into the river—for the first time, laws were set in stone. Babylonians knew the punishments for breaking public order, and the Code also declared that accused people were considered innocent until proven guilty.

C. 1750 BCE: BABYLONIAN ASTRONOMERS STUDY THE SKIES.

Around the time that Hammurabi ruled over Old Babylonia, astronomers watched the skies closely. By sight alone, they identified the visible planets and named constellations. Babylonians also traced the movements of the heavens, recognizing mathematical patterns in the changes. They recorded eclipses and even developed tables to calculate the movements of different celestial bodies.

The Babylonians linked their city's patron god, the mighty Marduk, to the planet Jupiter. As a result, they carefully tracked the path of Jupiter in the sky, making surprisingly accurate calculations without astronomical tools. Thousands of years ago, the Babylonians considered what lay beyond the earth, and found harmony in the heavens.

C. 1500 BCE: THE MAYA ESTABLISH THEIR CIVILIZATION IN CENTRAL AMERICA.

Rising from the jungles of Central America, the Maya developed writing and built massive stone pyramids. The civilization's first settlements date to around 1500 BCE, as villages slowly transformed into cities. In the highlands, Mayans planted maize and beans, while in the lowlands they fished in the Pacific Ocean. They also domesticated cacao, ushering in thousands of years of chocolate consumption.

The nearby Olmec culture became an important trading partner for the Maya. They traded precious objects like jade and obsidian. Both cultures also worshipped jaguars. As the centuries passed, the Maya inscribed monuments to their rulers and constructed elaborate cities that dominated an expansive empire.

C. 1490 BCE: IN EGYPT, HATSHEPSUT TAKES POWER AS ONE OF THE ONLY FEMALE PHARAOHS.

Pharaohs were supposed to be men—so when Hatshepsut took power in 1490 BCE, she donned men's clothes. Hatshepsut wasn't trying to hide her gender (her name means "First Among Noble Women"), but since the pharaohs of the past wore men's clothes, she adopted them as a symbol of power.

As a ruler, Hatshepsut built a massive temple and expanded Egypt's borders. She transformed the Valley of the Kings into a monumental burial site. After her death, Hatshepsut's successors tried to erase her name from history—and they nearly succeeded. Scholars in the 19th century discovered secret hieroglyphs that mentioned a female pharaoh. Today, Hatshepsut is seen as one of the greatest pharaohs in Egypt's long history.

C. 1400 BCE: THE CHINESE BEGIN TO USE CHOPSTICKS.

Europeans only began using forks in the 16th century, but for thousands of years, the Chinese had been using chopsticks. Around 1400 BCE, Shang Dynasty tombs buried rulers with bronze chopsticks. Cooks used chopsticks to fish noodles from boiling pots of water or dunk meat in hot oil. Wood and bamboo chopsticks likely existed even earlier than the expensive bronze and ivory chopsticks that appear in burial sites.

After the 5th century BCE, chopsticks became even more common. Confucius, who promoted a philosophy of non-violence, said "The honorable and upright man keeps well away from both the slaughterhouse and the kitchen. And he allows no knives on his table." In the place of knives, the Chinese ate with chopsticks.

C. 1300 BCE: IN THE PACIFIC, SEAFARERS REACH AND SETTLE NEW ZEALAND.

It's the greatest story of exploration in human history—for thousands of years, seafarers set off into the Pacific in their simple rafts and canoes. Using the stars as their guide, these seafarers settled in Fiji, the Polynesian Islands, and New Zealand. Spread over thousands of miles, voyagers discovered distant islands and returned home, maintaining trade routes that stretched across the ocean.

By 1300 BCE, seafarers had reached New Zealand, the last major landmass settled by humans. In their boats, they carried taro and sweet potato to the island, along with dogs. The settlers thrived in New Zealand and became the Māori people.

C. 1250 BCE: IN CHINA, ORACLE BONES PREDICT THE FUTURE.

In ancient China, fortune tellers carved complicated symbols into bones and then held them over flames until the bones cracked. The fortune teller then read the cracks to predict the future. These oracle bones provide the earliest written record of Chinese civilization—and their script evolved into today's modern Chinese language.

What kinds of questions did the ancient Chinese ask with oracle bones? The cracked bones helped people decide if they should have children, when to sell goods, and even whether they'd have a good day. Rulers asked their head diviners to use oracle bones to decide when to go to war. The diviners kept records of every question, the answer determined by the cracks, and if it came true.

1200 BCE: THE OLMEC RISE IN THE GULF OF MEXICO.

The Olmecs dominated the Gulf of Mexico around 1200 BCE. But where did they come from? The mysterious civilization did not even leave behind a name—the world "Olmec" comes from their successors, the Aztecs, who called the earlier civilization the "rubber people."

The Olmecs left behind evidence of their power. They traded rubber and fine pottery with their neighbors the Maya, and they also built stepped pyramids and ball-courts to play sports. The Olmec also carved jade and ceramic sculptures, which they sometimes buried in bogs. Although the mysterious Olmecs faded away, they influenced other mighty Mesoamerican civilizations like the Maya and Aztecs.

1000S BCE: THE PHOENICIANS INVENT AN INFLUENTIAL ALPHABET.

Mastering cuneiform or Egyptian hieroglyphics was a massive challenge—until a new innovation changed writing forever. Around 1000 BCE, the Phoenicians developed the first alphabet. Originally a simplified version of cuneiform, the Phoenician alphabet contained 22 letters. Phoenecian scribes wrote from right to left without vowels.

In 1000 BCE, the Phoenicians dominated the Mediterranean, setting up trading posts and traveling as far as the Atlantic Ocean to trade with other civilizations. As they traveled the Phoenicians also spread their alphabet. Today, scholars believe the Greeks borrowed their alphabet from the Phoenicians (adding in vowels), which makes it the ancestor of all Western alphabets. It also influenced the Aramaic alphabet which developed into modern Arabic.

C. 1000 BCE: THE OLMEC CARVE MASSIVE STONE HEADS.

Around 1000 BCE, the Olmec carved enormous stone heads—the largest towering over ten feet tall. They transported massive boulders up to 50 miles to create the heads. Even more surprisingly, the Olmec carved the heads without metal tools. Instead, stonemasons used stone hammers to sculpt the heads.

Why did the Olmecs carve these heads? Did they represent Olmec gods? Were they Olmec heroes? Today, archaeologists believe the heads represent Olmec rulers. Whatever their purpose, the Olmec buried the stone heads deep in the ground. The mysterious heads, which were originally decorated with bright colors, remained hidden until the 19th century—and even more may still be found buried under the earth.

THE RISE OF ANTIQUITY (800 BCE-400 BCE)

800 BCE: EGYPTIANS DEVELOP THE FIRST SURVIVING SUNDIAL.

Ancient Egyptians didn't just pioneer the solar calendar—they also developed the first surviving sundial around 800 BCE. Even before 800 BCE, the Egyptians marked time by tracing the shadow cast by obelisks.

Early sundials, drawn on limestone, divided the day into twelve sections. A raised bar cast a shadow onto the sundial, marking out the time. But because of the Earth's tilt, the length of an hour would be longer in summer than winter.

Why did ancient Egyptians need to keep time? One theory claims that a sundial discovered at the Valley of the Kings was used to schedule workers.

780 BCE: THE CHINESE RECORD A SOLAR ECLIPSE.

In the ancient world, a solar eclipse might signal disaster to people watching. When a solar eclipse took place in Syria around 1200 BCE., observers recorded the event on one side of a tablet and wrote "danger" on the other. After all, many ancient societies worshipped a powerful sun god, so the sun vanishing during the day might spell trouble.

In ancient China, imperial astronomers began recording eclipses around 780 BCE. For over 2,000 years, astronomers in China marked down nearly 1,000 solar eclipses. That dedication to recording observational data created an astonishingly accurate report for modern scholars.

776 BCE: THE FIRST OLYMPICS TAKE PLACE IN OLYMPIA, GREECE.

The Greek city of Olympia introduced a tradition that would last for centuries in 776 BCE. That year, the city-state held the first ever Olympic games. In 776 BCE, the games involved a single contest—a 192-meter race. The gold reportedly went to a cook named Coroebus, the first Olympic champion.

The Olympians continued to hold their games every four years, expanding the event to include new contests like the pentathlon, chariot racing, and wrestling. But the ancient Olympics weren't quite like the modern version. In its ancient version, the Olympic Games only allowed men to compete. And most athletes competed completely in the nude.

753 BCE: ROMULUS FOUNDS THE CITY OF ROME.

On April 21, 753 BCE, twin brothers stood atop the hills in Ancient Rome. The first, Romulus, wanted to found the city on the Palatine Hill, while his brother, Remus insisted on establishing the city on the Aventine Hill. Unable to compromise, Romulus began digging the foundation for his city wall. Remus mocked his brother and leaped over the wall. In response, Romulus killed his brother and named the city after himself: Rome.

For centuries, ancient Romans told the story of their city's founding as a warning to others never to mock the strength of Rome's walls—or its founder's commitment to defending the city.

C. 750 BCE: HOMER'S GREAT EPICS ARE WRITTEN DOWN FOR THE FIRST TIME.

"Tell me, Muse, of the man of many devices, who wandered far and wide after he had sacked Troy's sacred city, and saw the towns of many men and knew their mind." With this line, Homer began the *Odyssey*, an epic poem that defined ancient Greece. In the *Iliad* and the *Odyssey*, Homer captured what it meant to be Greek—chasing honor at any cost, remaining loyal to your allies, and demanding vengeance.

Around 750 BCE, as Greece emerged from a dark age, Homer's

works were written down for the first time. Was Homer a real person? Some claim he never existed. But whether a single person created the classic poems or a group of storytellers, Homer's works have shaped literature for centuries.

600 BCE: NEBUCHADNEZZAR BUILDS THE HANGING GARDENS OF BABYLON.

Though deserts dominate today's Middle East, 2600 years ago Babylon was a lush and powerful capital. Around 600 BCE, King Nebuchadnezzar II built the famous Hanging Gardens of Babylon to show off the capital. In an era when most growing focused on food, the Hanging Gardens emphasized pleasure.

Planted on raised platforms, trees and flowers spilled over their stone terraces, creating a waterfall of greenery. For centuries, ancient writers marveled over the gardens, deeming them one of the wonders of the ancient world. Like many of the other Seven Wonders of the Ancient World, the Hanging Gardens of Babylon no longer exist. Only the Great Pyramid of Giza still stands.

28 MAY 585 BC: GREEK PHILOSOPHER THALES CORRECTLY PREDICTS A SOLAR ECLIPSE.

On May 28, 585 BCE, the moon blocked out the sun. But this solar eclipse was different from the thousands that had come before. For the first time in history, a scientist predicted the eclipse before it took place. Thales of Miletus used records of previous solar eclipses to determine when the next would take place.

Thales's startlingly accurate prediction even ended a war, according to Herodotus, when the eclipse took place in the middle of a battle between the Medes and the Lydians. The prediction—and its confirmation—became one of the cardinal dates used to calculate other events in the ancient world.

513 BCE: FOR THE FIRST TIME, PEOPLE CREATE CAST IRON IN CHINA.

The world entered the Iron Age around 1200 BCE with the development of iron and steel. But a Chinese innovation in the 6th century BCE would push the Iron Age to new levels. Around 513 BCE, the Chinese made cast iron for the first time. Unlike the steel used in Europe and the Near East to create weapons, cast iron was perfectly suited to agriculture and cooking.

Much cheaper and easier to make than steel, even average people could afford a cast iron pot. As with many other innovations, the Chinese guarded the secret of cast iron, which didn't appear in Europe until the 15th century CE.

510 BCE: A GEOGRAPHER NAMED HECATEUS CREATES A MAP OF THE GREEK KNOWN WORLD.

In Miletus, a geographer drew a map in 510 BCE that captured the Greek view of the world. Hecateus placed Greece at the center of the known world, surrounded by a wheel of land. At the edges of the map, Hecateus placed the oceans.

When creating his map, Hecateus rejected stories and instead looked to eye-witnesses. "I write down what I think is true," he claimed, "because the stories told by the Greeks are, in my opinion, ridiculous and countless."

Herodotus described the map as "an Ocean flowing round the earth" with the land shown as "exactly circular," divided by the Mediterranean, the Red Sea, and the Black Sea. This Greek version of the world dominated geography for centuries.

5TH CENTURY BCE: GREEK PHILOSOPHERS WRITE THAT THE EARTH IS A SPHERE.

Around 500 BCE, Pythagoras wrote that the Earth was a sphere. How did the mathematician come to that conclusion? Did Pythagoras use mathematical calculations to disprove a flat Earth theory? A simpler explanation claims that he listened to sailors, who told tales of ships vanishing on the horizon.

However Pythagoras reached his conclusion, he shaped Greek philosophy for centuries—Plato and Aristotle both taught their students that the Earth was a sphere, and Eratosthenes used observations to determine the circumference of the planet.

As Plato explained, "My conviction is that the Earth is a round body in the center of the heavens." Aristotle added, "there are stars seen in Egypt and Cyprus which are not seen in the northerly regions," proving a spherical Earth.

490 BCE: A GREEK RUNS FROM THE CITY OF MARATHON TO ATHENS TO REPORT ON THE PERSIAN WAR.

An ancient Greek messenger named Phidippides took off running from Marathon to Athens in 490 BCE. The Persians had just invaded Greece, but the Greeks had managed a surprising victory over their powerful enemy. Phidippides covered the distance—about 25 miles—and reportedly dropped dead once he reached Athens.

The marathon reappeared in 1898 with the revival of the Olympic Games, and in the early 20th century the length of a marathon was officially set at 26.2 miles. But even though today's marathon takes its name from an ancient Greek feat of athletic endurance, the marathon never appeared in the ancient Olympic Games.

449 BCE: HERODOTUS, THE "FATHER OF HISTORY," WRITES A HISTORY OF THE PERSIAN WAR.

Herodotus wrote, "Of all men's miseries the bitterest is this, to know so much and to have control over nothing." In his *Histories*, Herodotus wrote the history of the Persian War and chronicled his travels to Egypt, Asia Minor, and Africa.

But Herodotus earned the title "father of history" for more than his book. Rather than using the Gods to explain events, Herodotus pointed to humans and their choices. But Herodotus didn't aim for perfect accuracy. Instead, he told stories about the past and invented dialogue and speeches to capture pivotal moments. Nearly 2,500 years later, Herodotus shapes how we think about the ancient world.

5TH CENTURY BCE: THE PERSIANS CREATE AN EFFICIENT POSTAL SYSTEM.

Couriers on horseback pushed their mounts to the limit to deliver the mail in ancient Persia. In the 5th century, the Persian Empire stretched from the Aegean to India, making it one of the largest empires the world had ever seen. And the Persians relied on their postal system to govern.

Thanks to Persia's postal system, rulers could send messages from Susa, near the Tigris River, to Sardis in western Turkey, in a single week. A man walking the same route would need three months to cross so much territory. From the capital of Persepolis, Persian emperors could send messages to India and Egypt using couriers who passed off messages with a relay system.

In awe of the Persian postal system, the Greek writer Xenophon called it the "fastest overland traveling on Earth." Herodotus marveled, "[They] are stopped neither by snow nor rain nor heat nor darkness"— a description that later became the motto of the U.S. Postal Service.

447 BCE: ATHENS BUILDS THE PARTHENON.

The brilliant statesman Pericles led Athens during its golden age. In 447 BCE, Athens built a new temple, dedicated to Athena and named the Parthenon. A magnificent example of ancient Greek architecture, the temple proclaimed Athens's status as the greatest city-state in Greece— at least, according to the Athenians.

But Athens's golden age came at a high cost to other Greek city-states. After the Persian War, Athens created a defensive league to protect Greece. Members were forced to pay fees to Athens, which led the league. When Pericles wanted to build a new temple, he simply took the money from the fund, building up Athens while letting the other city-states foot the bill.

C. 430 BCE: FIRST PERFORMANCE OF SOPHOCLES'S OEDIPUS REX.

In Ancient Greece, rich and poor crowded into open-air theaters to watch plays. And around 430 BCE, theatergoers saw the first performance of Sophocles's *Oedipus Rex*. Already considered a famous playwright, Sophocles had dazzled audiences with new innovations like expanding the chorus and adding painted scenery.

In his tragedies, Sophocles wanted to shock and disturb the audience. He captured how people's own choices often led them to tragic ends. In trying to avoid a prophecy, Oedipus and his parents end up fulfilling it, driving home the message that men must accept their fate. Or, in the words of Sophocles, "I have no desire to suffer twice, in reality and then in retrospect."

400 BCE: HIPPOCRATES FOUNDS AN INFLUENTIAL SCHOOL OF MEDICINE.

Today, doctors still take the Hippocratic Oath, vowing to "first, do no harm"—but who was Hippocrates? A famous physician born on the Greek island of Kos, Hippocrates opened a medical school and wrote dozens of influential books on medicine. His works taught physicians how to perform surgery, how different diseases progressed, and how to treat disorders.

Hippocrates encouraged observation and searching for natural rather than supernatural causes of diseases. As a result, many call Hippocrates the father of medicine. As for the Hippocratic Oath, it was probably written after Hippocrates died and named in honor of the illustrious physician.

THE BIRTH OF EMPIRES (400 BCE-200 BCE)

343 BCE: ARISTOTLE TUTORS A TEENAGED ALEXANDER THE GREAT IN MACEDON.

By 343 BCE, Aristotle had already earned the name "the man who knew everything." A Greek philosopher who promoted a systematic examination of knowledge, Aristotle's influence shaped science for nearly 2,000 years after his death.

A student of Plato, Aristotle became the tutor of Alexander the Great when he was the teenaged son of Philip II, King of Macedon. For seven years, Aristotle taught Alexander, until the boy became him himself.

When Alexander later conquered much of the known world, he carried Aristotle's works with him and introduced the Aristotelian philosophy to the Persians. Thanks to Alexander's success on the battlefield, Aristotle's works became even more influential.

323 BCE: ARISTOTLE FLEES ATHENS TO AVOID EXECUTION.

In 399 BCE, an Athenian jury executed Socrates for "refusing to recognize the gods recognized by the state" and "corrupting the youth." In 323 BCE, when Alexander the Great died, Aristotle fled Athens to avoid execution, quipping that he left "lest the Athenians sin twice against philosophy."

Aristotle's fears were valid—his mentor, Plato, had in turn been mentored by Socrates, and Athenians saw Alexander as a foreign conqueror. But Aristotle's escape didn't last long—he died of natural causes only a year later.

In the Middle Ages, Aristotle became known simply as "The

Master," for his writings on politics, medicine, biology, physics, mathematics, ethics, and logic.

320 BCE: THE LIBRARY AT ALEXANDRIA COLLECTS THE GREATEST WORKS OF ANTIQUITY.

Alexander the Great founded Alexandria in Egypt, and the city became one of the most important ports on the Mediterranean. As the capital of Ptolemaic Egypt, Alexandria was, to many, the greatest city in the ancient world. It also housed the greatest library in antiquity: the Library at Alexandria.

The library would hold a copy of every book in the world, its founders vowed. It eventually contained the works of Homer, Socrates, and Plato, making it one of the largest libraries in the ancient world. Scholars conducted research at the library, and the word "museum" comes from the library's Temple of Muses.

Centuries later, the Library at Alexandria burned to the ground, destroying the world's most complete collection of ancient literature.

312 BCE: ROMANS BUILD THEIR FIRST AQUEDUCT.

The Greeks were famous for their brains, while the Romans were famous for their drains. While Greek philosophy traveled the globe, the Romans undertook monumental and groundbreaking building projects—like the aqueducts.

The massive system of aqueducts transported freshwater across the empire. Using pipes, tunnels, and arched bridges, Romans brought fresh water to major cities like Rome, which had one of the most advanced plumbing systems in the world.

Starting around 312 BCE, the Romans began building the aqueducts, many of which would outlast their empire. In fact, a 2,000-year-old aqueduct still keeps Rome's Trevi Fountain running.

280 BCE: RHODES BUILDS ITS COLOSSUS

The bronze statue stood over 100 feet tall. Known as the Colossus of Rhodes, the massive monument to the sun god Helios marked the entrance to the harbor.

Instantly described as one of the Seven Wonders of the Ancient World, the statue didn't last long. In 226 BCE, an earthquake toppled the Colossus, leaving its broken remains sitting on the docks of Rhodes.

Even on the ground, the shattered statue impressed visitors. The Roman statesman Pliny the Elder marveled, "Few men can clasp the thumb in their arms, and its fingers are larger than most statues." Centuries later, people finally melted down the last pieces of the Colossus for scrap.

260 BCE: ARISTARCHUS OF SAMOS PROPOSES A HELIOCENTRIC MODEL.

Galileo got in trouble with the Catholic Church for claiming that the Sun, not the Earth, sat at the center of the universe. But he wasn't the first to find evidence of a heliocentric solar system in the heavens. Centuries earlier, Aristarchus of Samos argued that the Earth and the other planets actually revolved around the Sun.

A mathematician and astronomer, Aristarchus also believed the stars were themselves distant suns, making the universe much larger than anyone had previously believed. In his own time, most astronomers rejected Aristarchus's theories—but he was proved correct centuries after his death by men like Galileo.

250 BCE: ARCHIMEDES LEAPS OUT OF HIS BATH SHOUTING EUREKA.

On the island of Sicily, the engineer and inventor Archimedes took a bath 2,270 years ago – and that bath changed history. The King of Syracuse had ordered Archimedes to figure out if his new crown was actually pure gold. After failing to figure out a test, Archimedes stepped into a full bath, watching the water pour over the sides.

"Eureka!" Archimedes cried, leaping from the bath and running down the streets naked to test his new hypothesis. Archimedes had discovered buoyancy, the principle that the water displaced by an object will weigh the same as the object. He used the method to prove the crown wasn't pure gold after all.

220 BCE: THE GREEK MATHEMATICIAN ERATOSTHENES CALCULATES THE CIRCUMFERENCE OF THE WORLD.

For centuries, the Greeks knew the world was round—but how big was the Earth? Around 220 BCE, a Greek mathematician named Eratosthenes came up with a surprisingly accurate calculation. A scholar at the Library of Alexandria, Eratosthenes heard that in the southern city of Syene, men cast no shadows on the summer solstice. But the same wasn't true in Alexandria.

Eratosthenes measured the shadow in Alexandria and calculated its angle at 7.2 degrees. He then hired professional surveyors to calculate the distance between Syene and Alexandria. Using those numbers, Eratosthenes came up with a remarkably precise measurement of the circumference of the world.

202 BCE: LIU BANG FOUNDS THE HAN DYNASTY OF CHINA.

China's first emperor held on to power with an iron grip. Known for burning books and burying scholars—and monumental building projects like the Great Wall and the terracotta army—his overthrow ushered in the golden age of Ancient China.

In 202 BCE, Liu Bang founded the Han dynasty and became emperor. Born a peasant, Liu Bang led a rebellion against the previous emperor and rose to power while dodging assassination attempts.

Although he only ruled for seven years, the Han dynasty continued for four centuries. During China's golden age, the Han dynasty devoted itself to Confucianism, opened the Silk Road, and promoted key innovations like paper.

200 BCE: THE NAZCA CREATE LARGE-SCALE EARTH DRAWINGS.

Enormous hummingbirds, lizards, dogs, and fish appear in a Peruvian desert. Carved into the earth, the mysterious symbols, called the Nazca lines today, trace hundreds of miles across a dry plateau. The Nazca lines represent some of the largest man-made art in history—and they were created over 2,000 years ago.

Why did the Nazca create these monumental shapes? One theory claims the figures represent constellations, while another argues the Nazca used the lines as enormous looms to create long woven textiles. Did the Nazca trace underground water sources with the lines, or were they ceremonial? Most believe the lines were religious, a way to connect the Nazca to their gods in the heavens. The mystery over the Nazca lines continues to fascinate people today.

THE GOLDEN AGE OF EMPIRES (200 BCE-200 CE)

196 BCE: THE ROSETTA STONE TRANSLATES EGYPTIAN HIEROGLYPHS.

Ptolemy V, the ruler of Egypt, ordered his followers to carve a message into an enormous black slab in 196 BCE. The decree, posted in every Egyptian temple, declared that the region's priests supported Ptolemy. To make sure everyone could read the decree, the Rosetta stone copied the same message in three scripts: ancient Greek, Demotic, and hieroglyphs.

Egyptians used these scripts for different purposes. Administrators used Greek, the language of the conqueror Alexander the Great. In daily life, Egyptians used Demotic. And hieroglyphs were still used for priestly decrees, even thousands of years after Egypt's greatest pharaohs died. What makes the Rosetta stone so important? In the 19th century, it helped scholars crack the code of the hieroglyphs, which had been lost centuries earlier.

100 BCE: ON THE ISLAND OF MILO, A SCULPTOR CARVES A VENUS.

In the 19th century, a Greek peasant named Yorgos stumbled upon an ancient marble statue while plowing his field. Although the statue had lost its arms, it instantly became one of the most recognizable sculptures in history: the Venus de Milo. Centuries later, the Venus de Milo remains, for many, the ideal of female beauty.

Who made the Venus de Milo, and what did the statue look like with her arms? Scholars believe a sculptor created the statue of Aphrodite on the Greek island of Milo around 100 BCE. The statue's marble skin looked different in the Hellenistic era when it was first made: the sculptor likely draped the statue in jewelry and added colored paint to make it look life-like.

49 BCE: JULIUS CAESAR CROSSES THE RUBICON RIVER AND TAKES THE CITY OF ROME.

What does it mean to cross the Rubicon? The famous metaphor, which means taking a decisive step with no going back. The phrase comes from Julius Caesar, who led his army across the Rubicon river north of Rome in 49 BCE. In ancient Rome, bringing an army into Italy was treason. The republic feared military strength would turn elected rulers into dictators.

When Caesar reached the Rubicon with his troops, he stopped to weigh his options. If he left his army into the Italian peninsula, he faced arrest from the Senate and exile. But crossing the river would start a civil war. Caesar ultimately declared, "let the die be cast!" and rode on to Rome. Crossing the Rubicon triggered five years of civil war and Caesar's assassination.

48 BCE: CLEOPATRA RISES AS EGYPT'S SOLE RULER.

Cleopatra battled family and beat the odds to take control of Egypt in 48 BCE. After her brother and husband Ptolemy XIII drove Cleopatra from Alexandria, she hatched a plan to return to power. The Roman ruler Julius Caesar had just arrived in Egypt, where he ordered the warring siblings to appear before him. When Ptolemy barred Cleopatra from attending, she hid in a rolled-up carpet to smuggle herself into Caesar's rooms.

When Cleopatra tumbled out of the carpet, she won over the Roman, who supported her ascent. But relying on Romans for assistance ultimately backfired when, nearly two decades later, Cleopatra committed suicide to avoid capture from Julius Caesar's heir Octavian.

27 BCE: OCTAVIAN BECOMES THE LIFE-LONG RULER OF ROME AND TAKES THE NAME AUGUSTUS.

When a cabal of Senators assassinated Julius Caesar in 44 BCE, the ruler left behind a teenage heir. That boy, Octavian, spent the rest of his life avenging Caesar's death. In 27 BCE, after a long war against his main rival Mark Antony, Octavian became Rome's first emperor and took the name Augustus Caesar.

But Augustus carefully maintained the myth of the Roman Republic, wary of the opposition Julius faced. As a result, Augustus never called himself emperor. Instead, he used the title *Princeps*, or "first citizen." He devoted his decades of rule to "restoring the Republic," even while he reigned as emperor.

27 BCE: LIVY BEGINS WRITING HIS HISTORY OF ROME.

Rome had experienced over two decades of civil war when a historian named Livy decided to write a history of Rome. Livy's work chronicled the founding of Rome and the establishment of the Roman Republic through the rise of Augustus Caesar.

But Livy wrote more than Rome's history. He chronicled the rise and fall of Roman virtue. Livy argued that the empire would only survive if Romans returned to their founding virtues. In his own time, Livy worried, "We can endure neither our vices nor the remedies for them." If Romans neglected traditional rituals and institutions, Rome would suffer.

Or, as Livy put it, "The study of history is the best medicine for a sick mind; for in history you have a record of the infinite variety of human experience plainly set out for all to see: and in that record you can find for yourself and your country both examples and warnings: fine things to take as models, base things, rotten through and through, to avoid."

1 CE: LIONS BECOME EXTINCT IN EUROPE.

For centuries, lions roamed Europe. Ancient Greeks wrote about heroes who battled lions and ancient Romans hunted lions. But around 1 CE, lions vanished from Europe and never returned.

What drove lions to extinction? Excessive hunting was a major factor, since both the Greeks and Romans enjoyed lion hunting. Lions also faced fierce competition from feral dogs and shrinking territories.

Even after lions went extinct in Europe, the Romans imported lions to fight in their arenas. In front of massive audiences, lions battled against other animals like bears and tigers. The Romans also punished criminals by throwing them to the lions. But after 1 CE, Romans had to look for lions in North Africa and the Middle East.

2 CE: CHINA CONDUCTS A POPULATION CENSUS.

In 2 CE, one in every four people on the planet lived in China. That year, the Han Dynasty conducted a census that recorded nearly 60 million people. Although Chinese censuses date back at least 1,000 years before the Han census, the 2 CE count is the oldest census where records still survive today.

Although China boasted the world's largest population in 2 CE, it didn't have the world's largest city. Though 250,000 people lived in the Chinese capital of Chang'an, Rome had China beat on city size. In the 1st century, Rome became the first city to hit a population of one million people.

8 CE: OVID WRITES POETRY--AND AUGUSTUS EXILES HIM FROM ROME.

"Let others praise ancient times," wrote the Roman poet Ovid. "I am glad I was born in these." Ovid became Rome's most famous poet, writing the epic *Metamorphoses* that chronicled the history of the world, beginning with its creation and ending with the already mythical figure of Julius Caesar.

But Ovid ran into trouble with Rome's emperor Augustus for another poem, called *The Art of Love*. In it, Ovid told men—and women—how to seduce members of the opposite sex. The scandalous work offended Augustus, who promoted traditional virtues as Rome's ruler, even passing marriage laws to encourage monogamy. In 8 CE, Augustus banished Ovid to the edge of the empire. That didn't stop Ovid, who still believed "Fortune and love favor the brave."

14 CE: AUGUSTUS DIES AFTER DECADES RULING ROME.

On his deathbed, Augustus Caesar declared, "I found Rome a city of clay but left it a city of marble." During his decades as Rome's ruler, Augustus built temples, Roman baths, and theaters. He also invested in the arts and promised to bring Rome back to its republican foundations.

Yet with his death, many Romans wondered if Rome's golden age had ended. Would Rome return to its republican form of government, or would the empire continue? Was Augustus a singular figure or would there be more emperors after his death? Augustus himself wanted his adopted son Tiberius to rule as emperor—and Augustus's rule ushered in centuries of imperial rule in Rome.

C. 20 CE: CHINESE ASTRONOMER LIU XIN CATALOGS OVER 1,000 DIFFERENT STARS.

As the Han dynasty's imperial librarian, Liu Xin cataloged every star Chinese astronomers had noted in the heavens. In total, his catalog contained 1,080 stars. But Liu Xin was more than a librarian. As a scholar, he calculated the value of pie to four digits, annotated dozens of ancient texts, and wrote historical texts. He also founded a school of Confucianism.

Liu Xin's close relationship with imperial power ended, however, when he participated in a Han-backed plot to overthrow the usurper emperor Wang Mang. Although the plot was unsuccessful and led to Liu Xin's death, the Han emerged victorious just one month later.

C. 29 CE: JESUS BEGINS HIS MINISTRY IN JUDEA.

"Do not let your hearts be troubled," preached Jesus, "Trust in God; trust also in me." Around 29 CE, John the Baptist baptized Jesus in the River Jordan, beginning Jesus's rise as a prophet. In his sermons, Jesus taught his followers through stories that emphasized loving one's neighbors, caring for the poor, and forgiving one's enemies.

While scholars disagree on some of the specifics in the New Testament accounts of Jesus, they agree on three things: Jesus was an actual, historical figure; he was baptized by John the Baptist; and he was ultimately crucified. The message Jesus carried continues to shape the world 2,000 years later.

31 CE: CHINESE ENGINEER DU SHI INVENTS THE FIRST HYDRAULIC-POWERED BELLOWS.

The Han dynasty continued its technological innovations with the invention of water-powered bellows. Engineer Du Shi was the first to use a water wheel to power bellows used to cast iron. Watermills themselves were an invention of the Han dynasty that helped feed a country of over 60 million people by grinding grain.

In the 5th century, a historian explained Du Shi's invention and reported, "the people got great benefit for little labor. They found the 'water bellows' convenient and adopted it widely." Thanks to the labor-saving devices, which were mainly used to improve agricultural efficiency, China could sustain the world's largest population.

41 CE: A SRI LANKAN AMBASSADOR NAMED RACHIAS TRAVELS TO ROME.

When a storm in the Indian Ocean swept a Roman trader off course, he landed in Sri Lanka and met King Bhatikabhaya in the Sinhalese court. Curious about the far-off Roman Empire, the king sent an embassy to Emperor Claudius to make an alliance. The head ambassador, called Rachias by the Romans or Raki by the Sri Lankans, reached Rome around 41 CE.

Rachias carried tales of the "silk people" in the far East and the riches of India. Roman senators held up the Sinhalese system of government as a subtle criticism of their emperor. And contact between the two continued, with Roman ships sailing to Sri Lanka for several centuries.

50 CE: BUDDHIST MONKS IN SRI LANKA FIRST WRITE DOWN BUDDHA'S TEACHINGS.

It took 500 years for the followers of the Buddha, or "Enlightened One," to write down his teaching. Though the Buddha died in the 5th century, Buddhist scripture was passed down orally in India. At the time, writing was rare, so followers memorized discourses to spread his message of karma, rebirth, and spiritual enlightenment.

Around 50 CE, Buddhist monks in Sri Lanka became the first to write down Buddhist scripture. At the time, famine and conflict threatened to destroy Buddhist communities, making it more important than ever to record the Buddha's teaching. Using the Pāli language, the monks created the oldest Buddhist scriptures, divided into the words of the Buddha, monastic rules, and scholastic texts.

60 CE: BOUDICCA LEADS A REBELLION AGAINST THE ROMANS.

She set fire to London to defend her land. The Celtic queen Boudicca led a massive revolt against the Romans in Britain. Boudicca was fighting for her way of life and her daughters—according to Roman rules, only men could lead. "Nothing is safe from Roman pride and arrogance," Boudicca proclaimed. "Win the battle or perish, that is what I, a woman, will do."

Boudicca led tens of thousands of rebels in her battle against the Romans. After a series of victories, the Romans overwhelmed the rebels with their military might. Though she eventually fell, a statue of Boudicca stands next to Parliament in London today.

70 CE: PLINY THE ELDER BEGINS WRITING HIS NATURAL HISTORY.

"In these matters, the only certainty is that nothing is certain," wrote Pliny the Elder in his *Natural History*, an ambitious ten-volume work dedicated to understanding the world. A Roman administrator and scientist, Pliny investigated the world and recorded Roman knowledge on geography, biology, agriculture, and mathematics.

For centuries, scholars pointed to Pliny as the authority on the natural world. His efforts to capture all ancient knowledge also inspired later encyclopedias. Pliny died before completing his work. When Vesuvius erupted in 79 CE, he led an evacuation effort in Pompeii. But the relief efforts ended up costing Pliny his life.

79 CE: MOUNT VESUVIUS ERUPTS, DESTROYING POMPEII AND HERCULANEUM.

It was one of the most violent natural disasters in the ancient world. When Mount Vesuvius erupted in 79 CE, it buried the cities of Pompeii and Herculaneum under a thick layer of mud and ash. "Some bewailed their own fate," wrote Pliny the Younger, who watched the eruption from the Bay of Naples. "Others prayed to die." The eruption killed his father, Pliny the Elder.

But the eruption also perfectly preserved two important Roman cities, freezing them for later scholars to study. The frescoes and mosaics of Pompeii provide a window into the past, helping people today understand life during the height of Rome's power nearly 2,000 years ago.

80 CE: IN ROME, THE COLOSSEUM IS FINISHED.

When the Romans finished building the Colosseum in 80 CE, they celebrated with 100 days of gladiator fights. The massive four-story arena could hold 50,000 Romans and dwarfed every other arena in the empire. For centuries, Roman emperors rewarded their loyal subjects by hosting spectacular events in the Colosseum.

On the arena floor, wild animals battled each other and gladiators clashed as crowds cheered. The Romans used secret trap doors to release lions into the area and even flooded the entire arena to host naval battles. The Colosseum also held public executions for convicted criminals.

From its monumental size to its blood sports, the Colosseum represents the Roman commitment to *panem et circenses*—bread and circuses—by keeping the public happy with cheap food and entertainment.

98 CE: TACITUS WRITES GERMANIA.

The Romans were fascinated with the Germanic tribes who lived on the northern border of their empire. In 98 CE, the Roman politician and historian Tacitus wrote a book dedicated to the Germanic tribes. But *Germania* was not a neutral assessment of the tribes. Instead, Tacitus criticized Rome by comparing their "civilized" behavior with that of the "savage" Germans.

"No one in Germany laughs at vice," wrote Tacitus, "nor do they call it the fashion to corrupt and to be corrupted." In Germany, wives were monogamous and men didn't turn to the pleasures of the Roman baths or the banquets. By holding up the Germanic tribes as a mirror, Tacitus captured the Roman fear that their luxuries were destroying the empire.

100: IN INDIA, A CHOLA KING BUILDS AN ANCIENT DAM KNOWN AS THE GRAND ANICUT.

For over 1,500 years, the Chola dynasty controlled southern India. As rulers, the Chola invested in art and literature, creating bronze sculptures and elaborate temples. Around 100 CE, a Chola king built a massive dam across the Kaveri River to irrigate the land and control flooding. That dam, known as the Grant Anicut or Kallanai Dam, still works nearly 2,000 years later.

Centuries after building the dam, the Chola expanded their territory, conquering Sri Lanka and sending invading ships overseas to the Maldives, Malaysia, Indonesia, and Southern Thailand. Although the invasions ultimately failed, Chola explorers created new trading routes in the Indian Ocean and spread Chola culture throughout the region.

100: ROMANS BEGIN WORSHIPING THE EGYPTIAN GODDESS ISIS.

The goddess Isis saved her husband, Osiris, from death and raised the first pharaoh. Egyptians worshipped Isis for centuries, but after Rome conquered the Nile River Valley, Isis became a major figure in Roman religion. Although Augustus rejected the cult of Isis as foreign, later Roman emperors worshipped the Egyptian goddess. Temples to Isis dotted the empire and Romans set up private shrines in their homes.

The popularity of Isis at the height of the Roman Empire may seem surprising—but the Romans were more likely to incorporate the gods of their subject states into their pantheon than ban them completely. With

Rome controlling the entire Mediterranean, an Egyptian goddess symbolized the empire's cosmopolitan reach.

105: CAI LUN OF CHINA INVENTS PAPER.

One day, Emperor He handed a court official named Cai Lun a stack of documents carved into bamboo strips. As Cai Lun struggled to carry the cartful of documents home, he wondered if he could create a better alternative to the heavy and awkward bamboo strips. At home, Cai Lun experimented with hemp fibers, tree bark, cloth, and silk cocoons, which he blended and cooked. After cooking, Cai Lun pounded the ingredients into a starchy paste until he created paper.

The inventor presented his paper to the emperor, who instantly declared it a success. Cai Lun earned the title Marquis of Dragon Pavilion and his invention took the name Marquis Cai paper.

120: EMPEROR HADRIAN OVERSEES THE BUILDING OF THE PANTHEON IN ROME.

When Emperor Hadrian came to power in 117, he vowed to leave behind monumental buildings to rival his predecessors. In the 120s, he built one of the most magnificent buildings from ancient Rome: the Pantheon. Originally a Roman temple, the Pantheon boasted a 142-foot dome with a 27-foot oculus in the center.

By the 7th century, the Pantheon became a Christian church, and by the Renaissance, it inspired architects like Michelangelo to revive the classical design of its dome. The largest dome in the world until the 15th century, today the Pantheon remains the largest solid concrete dome in the world. Ironically, instead of putting his own name on the Pantheon's portico, Hadrian labeled it for Marcus Agrippa, a Roman consul from the 1st century BCE.

122: THE ROMANS BUILD HADRIAN'S WALL IN NORTHERN ENGLAND.

The Celtic warriors of Scotland were so fierce that Emperor Hadrian feared they might overrun Roman Britain. Around 122, the Romans built an enormous wall to divide Britain into two sections. The stone fortification called Hadrian's Wall covered 73 miles of land, dotted with forts and ditches, to stop the Celts from raiding into Roman Britain.

Stretching from one coast of Britain to the other, Hadrian's Wall showed a new side of the Romans. Rather than focusing on conquest, the empire now worried about defense. The wall marked the northernmost outpost of the Roman Empire, but by the 4th century, Roman emperors were withdrawing from Britain as their empire drastically contracted.

132: ZHANG HENG OF CHINA INVENTS THE FIRST SEISMOMETER TO DETECT EARTHQUAKES.

When earthquakes shook China, the Han Dynasty sent aid as quickly as possible. But if natural disasters disrupted communications, the empire didn't always know when help was needed. In 132, Zhang Heng solved that problem by creating a seismometer that could detect earthquakes and even point to the direction of the quake.

Zhang Heng's invention reported earthquakes from hundreds of miles away. In one case, the seismometer reported a quake when members of the court felt nothing. Just days later, a runner arrived to confirm that an earthquake hit a village 400 miles away. Zhang Heng was more than an inventor and scientist. He also wrote innovative poems.

160: APULEIUS, A ROMAN WRITER, WRITES THE GOLDEN ASS.

On a trip to Greece, Lucius experimented with magic and turned himself into a donkey. In Apuleius's 2nd century novel, Lucius the donkey crosses the Roman empire searching for an antidote. He runs into con-men dressed as priests, gets attacked by rabid dogs, and escapes with runaway slaves—just to run into armed farmers. When one of his many owners tries to eat Lucius, he barely escapes with his life.

Finally, the goddess Isis transforms Lucius back into a man—with a promise that he will dedicate his life to the gods. The novel captured Rome at its height, when a traveler could cross 2,000 miles speaking the same language.

161: MARCUS AURELIUS BECOMES ROMAN EMPEROR.

"You have power over your mind—not outside events," wrote Marcus Aurelius in his *Meditations*. "Realize this, and you will find strength." As the last of Rome's Five Good Emperors, Marcus Aurelius blended his political power with philosophy, writing on the purpose of life and ethics. Aurelius ruled according to his philosophy by placing the common good above all else.

As a Stoic, Aurelius believed that life's ups and downs were natural. He avoided self-pity and accepted tragedy as part of life. As Aurelius wrote, "fear of death is fear of what we may experience: nothing at all or something quite new. But if we experience nothing, we can experience nothing bad. And if our experience changes, then our existence changes with it – change, but not cease."

170: CLAUDIUS PTOLEMY WRITES INFLUENTIAL WORKS IN ASTRONOMY, ASTROLOGY, AND GEOGRAPHY.

In the 2nd century, an Egyptian geographer named Claudius Ptolemy drew a map of the world. Ptolemy's map used the system of latitude and longitude to record the precise location of 8,000 places, stretching from the Shetland Islands to the Pacific Ocean. By bringing together everything the Romans knew about the world during the empire's height, Ptolemy created the most influential ancient world map.

But Ptolemy also turned his attention to the skies, writing astronomical works that described the Ptolemaic, or geocentric, theory of the universe. For 1,300 years after his death, Ptolemy's writings on the world and the heavens shaped science.

184: PEASANTS RISE UP IN THE YELLOW TURBAN REBELLION IN CHINA.

While Han rulers presided over a corrupt court, peasants in China starved—until the Yellow Turbans, a secret society, led a rebellion against the Han. The rebels donned yellow headdresses and gained thousands of followers by claiming the Han dynasty had lost the

Mandate of Heaven, or divine support. They also used poetry and public criticism to attack the Han dynasty.

For two decades, the underground Yellow Turban Rebellion plagued the Han dynasty. Although the government eventually stamped out the movement, the dynasty soon fell, splintering China into warring fragments. As one of the only nationwide peasant uprisings in China, the Yellow Turbans shaped the country's history.

193: THE YEAR OF THE FIVE EMPERORS IN ROME.

On New Year's Eve in 192, a wrestler strangled Emperor Commodus in his bath. Over the next year, five different men would claim imperial power in Rome, leaving the empire in chaos.

Rome's first of the five emperors lasted three months—until the Senate plotted to assassinate him. The second emperor bribed his way into office but was murdered before summer. Civil war broke out between the third, fourth, and fifth emperors, who seized different parts of Rome's massive empire. One was killed while fleeing Rome, another was assassinated, and the final emperor, Septimius Severus, ruled Rome for nearly two decades.

The instability of the Year of the Five Emperors was only a warning of what was to come to Rome. During the Third Century Crisis, dozens of men plotted, schemed, and killed to seize power, weakening the empire.

199: GALEN, ONE OF THE MOST INFLUENTIAL ANCIENT PHYSICIANS, DIES.

Galen studied human anatomy up close—as a physician for Roman gladiators. Understanding anatomy was the key to treating patients, Galen believed. By studying the structure of the heart, the flow of blood, and the effects of disease on the body, physicians could heal more patients. The key to medicine, according to Galen, was balance. If the body was out of balance, it became weak and vulnerable to diseases and illnesses like cancer.

While some of Galen's conclusions were flawed or incomplete, his dedication to anatomy and medicine built a powerful legacy for Galen.

For 1,500 years, his theories on the body and medicine shaped medical treatments in Europe.

200: IN THE PERUVIAN ANDES, PEOPLE CULTIVATE A HIGH ELEVATION POTATO.

In the foothills of the Andes, ancient Peruvians planted maize, squash, and beans. But these crops withered and died in the mountain's higher altitudes. On the plateaus 14,000 feet above sea level, few crops could survive. Freezing temperatures, harsh sun, and low oxygen levels made the Andes almost uninhabitable—until ancient Peruvians cultivated a high-altitude potato.

In the highlands of the Andes, farmers planted potatoes underground, protecting them from frigid conditions. These hearty potatoes could resist frost and disease, allowing people to thrive high into the mountains. Along with a high-elevation potato, people also cultivated peanuts and quinoa. Centuries later, these crops allowed the Inca to create a massive empire in South America.

212: ROME BEGINS CONSTRUCTION ON THE BATHS OF CARACALLA.

The Romans loved their baths, and in 212 the emperor Caracalla began building the most magnificent baths in the empire. Caracalla forced 13,000 Scottish prisoners of war to build his baths. They created a four-story structure fed by a new aqueduct. Below the baths, a crew of hundreds threw ten tons of wood into the furnaces every day to heat the water.

The Baths of Caracalla could serve 1,600 people at once in its many cold, tepid, and hot baths. The facility's open-air bath matched the dimensions of a modern Olympic swimming pool. As part of the luxurious experience, Romans could also visit massage rooms, perfumeries, and a hair salon on the grounds.

Luxury had become a way of life for the Romans. As one Roman wrote in his epitaph, "Baths, wine, and sex spoil our bodies; but baths, wine, and sex make up life."

250: THE MAYA CIVILIZATION BEGINS ITS CLASSICAL ERA.

In the 3rd century, the Maya classical era began. During the golden age of the Maya, 40 cities flourished in Central America with a total population of around 2 million. They painted sacred temples with mica to make them sparkle and aligned their step pyramids with the stars. Kings and queens carved their names on the walls of pyramids using a complicated system of hieroglyphs.

But the Maya also conquered neighbors and practiced human sacrifice. They created one of the first team sports, where players competed to toss a heavy ball through a hoop. But the stakes in the game were much more than bragging rights. The losing team was sacrificed to the gods.

274: ZENOBIA RULES AS QUEEN OF THE PALMYRENE EMPIRE IN SYRIA

Her ancestors included Cleopatra and Dido of Carthage—or, at least, that's what Queen Zenobia of the Palmyrene Empire claimed. She spoke Greek, Latin, Egyptian, and Aramaic, and Zenobia led her troops into battle. Her empire connected the Silk Road to Rome, making it an important trade center. While the Romans burned through 26 emperors in half a century, Zenobia seized control of Egypt. She also expanded her influence into Asia Minor until her empire swallowed up a third of Rome.

Challenging Roman rule earned Zenobia powerful enemies. Soon, a Roman army descended on Syria, forcing Zenobia to flee. She nearly escaped to Persia before the Romans brought Zenobia back to their capital—where a jury acquitted her and she lived out the rest of her days in luxury.

284: AFTER DECADES OF DISORDER, DIOCLETIAN BECOMES ROMAN EMPEROR.

Revolts, rebellions, and invasions left Rome weak and fractured in the 3rd century. But when Diocletian rose to power in 284, he stabilized the empire by dividing power between four co-emperors. This system created a senior and junior emperor in the eastern and western halves of the empire, an echo of the Roman Republic's two consul system.

The Roman empire's massive size was part of its undoing. No single emperor could hope to control a territory that took weeks to cross. But Diocletian's system of divided imperial power barely outlasted his rule. When Diocletian stepped down, civil war broke out until a new emperor emerged victorious: Constantine.

LATE ANTIQUITY (300-600)

318: IN ROME, CHRISTIANS FOUND THE FIRST ST. PETER'S CHURCH.

The Romans had a flexible view of religion. They borrowed their gods from the Greeks and incorporated Egyptian gods like Isis into their pantheon. But the Romans drew the line at monotheistic faiths. Until Emperor Constantine converted to Christianity and threw his support behind the religion.

Around 318, on Constantine's orders, Christians built a great basilica in Rome, named after St. Peter. The basilica's walls contained frescoes showing the Apostles and Biblical scenes—plus a mosaic of Constantine. For centuries, St. Peter's Basilica became one of the most important churches in Christendom. Dozens of papal coronations took place in the church, which became a major pilgrimage destination. Although Constantine moved Rome's capital to the east, he helped turn Rome into the capital of the Catholic church.

322: CHINA INVENTS THE STIRRUP

Before the stirrup, riding a horse into war could prove deadly. In the 6th century BCE, a Persian king died when he accidentally stabbed himself while mounting his horse. But everything changed in the 4th century when the Chinese invented the stirrup.

The simple foot support, attached to a saddle, gave riders more control on horseback. Archers could fire arrows from the back of a horse with much greater precision. Cavalrymen could carry lances into battle.

· · ·

The first stirrups were made from bronze or cast iron. For centuries, China alone benefitted from the technological advancement, but by the 8th century, the stirrup had reached the Mediterranean and Europe.

330: CONSTANTINE THE GREAT MOVES ROME'S CAPITAL

By the 4th century, Rome was in decline. The building projects of earlier emperors were falling into disrepair. So the new Roman emperor decided to move the capital to a new city, which he named after himself: Constantinople.

Why did Constantine move the capital? The eastern half of the Roman empire was much richer than its western half, so the new capital surrounded the emperor in luxury. Constantinople's bay offered more protection than Rome, and the harbor made it a trading center.

Plus, Constantine wanted something new. Rather than building on the ruins of a millennium of history, he designed a capital from scratch. In the following centuries, Constantinople became one of the mightiest cities in the world.

360: THE FIRST MONASTERY IN WESTERN EUROPE BEGINS AT LIGUGÉ.

Monasteries became important centers of knowledge in medieval Europe. But the concept first started in Egypt. Christians in the Near East wanted a place to withdraw from society to contemplate religion. The idea quickly spread throughout Christendom, and in 360 a French community called Ligugé established the first monastery in western Europe.

At first, the French monastery copied Egyptian monks, who each lived in a small hut. But soon European monasteries moved toward communal living following a code of rules. In the 6th century, Benedict of Nursia created the Benedictine order, encouraging monks to live a simple, self-sufficient life devoted to prayer and religious study.

393: EMPEROR THEODOSIUS ENDS THE ANCIENT GAMES OF OLYMPIA.

The ancient Olympic games continued for over a thousand years, pushing athletes to show off their abilities. But in 393, Emperor Theodosius ended the games. Rome, which was now a Christian empire, didn't see the need for a contest dedicated to the Greek gods. Theodosius also banned pagan rituals across the empire.

Rome's economic situation had also changed by the 4th century. The empire could no longer afford to pay for expensive festivals. Many, like the Olympics, were so costly that private Romans chose not to shoulder the economic burden.

But the spirit of the Olympics continued outside of Olympia. In Ephesus, athletes continued to compete into the 5th century, and Antioch held a version of the Olympics until the 6th century.

395: HYPATIA BUILDS A REPUTATION FOR HER ACHIEVEMENTS IN PHILOSOPHY AND MATHEMATICS.

Hypatia of Alexandria put on a scholar's robe and strode to the city center. In a public square, she lectured on Plato and Aristotle, educating men and women about nature. Hypatia was one of the greatest mathematicians and astronomers of the era. The daughter of a math professor, she studied astronomy and science before giving her own lectures.

As an adult, Hypatia became one of the first female professors at the University of Alexandria. But she made powerful enemies. The city's new Christian rulers accused Hypatia of witchcraft. In 415, after giving a lecture at the university, a mob of monks killed Hypatia and the university was burned to the ground.

397: AUGUSTINE OF HIPPO BEGINS WRITING HIS CONFESSIONS.

"Men go abroad to admire the heights of mountains, the mighty waves of the sea, the broad tides of rivers, the compass of the ocean, and the circuits of the stars," wrote Augustine of Hippo in his *Confessions*, "Yet [men] pass over the mystery of themselves without a thought."

In his autobiographical work, Augustine recounted every sinful deed from his youth. He stole pears from a garden. He believed in astrology. He struggled with lust. These sins, Augustine came to believe after converting to Christianity, all came from man's original sin and his sinful nature.

By cataloging his immorality, Augustine encouraged readers to look at their own lives and convert to Christianity.

399: FAXIAN WALKS FROM CHINA TO INDIA IN SEARCH OF BUDDHIST SCRIPTURES.

In 399, a Chinese Buddhist monk named Faxian set out from China to walk to India. The journey took three years on foot. But when Faxian reached India, he found precious Buddhist texts that weren't available in China. The monk continued his journey throughout India and spent two years in Sri Lanka learning more.

On his journey home, Faxian boarded a ship and sailed to Java before traveling back to China. After completing his long, dangerous trip, Faxian spent the rest of his life writing about Buddhism and what he saw along the Silk Road, in India, and in Java. He also devoted himself to translating Buddhist texts into Chinese.

400: IN THE NORTH AMERICAN PLAINS, THE BOW AND ARROW REPLACE THE SPEAR.

For centuries, Native Americans in the great plains used spears to hunt bison and fight their enemies. These spears contained a stone tip tied to a wooden handle. Hunters even perfected throwing spears at animals. But in the 5th century, a new weapon replaced the spear: the bow and arrow.

Great Plains hunters learned of the bow and arrow from hunters who lived to the north in Canada's arctic. The bow and arrow offered several advantages. Hunters could fire at targets from a distance with much greater precision. Creating stone arrowheads took less time than making spear tips. And arrows were smaller and lighter, making them more mobile. The technological advancement transformed life on the Great Plains.

400: TIKAL, ONE OF THE GREATEST MAYA CITIES, BUILDS THE NORTH ACROPOLIS.

The city of Tikal in Central America became one of the most powerful Maya cities in the classical era—all without a source of fresh water. While building monumental pyramids, temples, and palaces, the people of Tikal also created enormous underground cisterns that caught rainwater. Drinking only water that fell from the sky, Tikal sustained a population of 100,000 people at its height.

Around 400, the people of Tikal expanded their royal acropolis, adding four towering pyramids. The massive building project points to a thriving city. But the Maya abandoned cities like Tikal around the 10th century. Today, some scholars believe droughts pushed the Maya to abandon cities that relied on rainwater.

410: THE VISIGOTHS SACK ROME

When Romulus founded Rome in 753 BCE, he vowed that no one would breach the city's wall. That promise held for over a thousand years. But in 410 CE, the Visigoths sacked Rome. An army of 40,000 swarmed through the Salarian Gate, where they burned temples, looted palaces, and hauled off gold and silver.

The Visigoths, who had converted to Christianity, left Rome's churches untouched and spared refugees inside the churches.

Horrified Romans looked for the cause of their great city's decline. Some pointed to the empire's recent adoption of Christianity, which had angered the Roman gods. Others blamed pagans who refused to bow to Christianity.

421: ACCORDING TO LEGEND, ROMANS FLEEING VISIGOTHS FOUND THE CITY OF VENICE.

In the 5th century, Germanic tribes overran the western Roman empire. The Vandals, Visigoths, Huns, and Ostrogoths swarmed into France, Spain, and Italy. Tribal rulers set up new kingdoms within Rome's boundaries, threatening to destroy the once-mighty empire. The

Vandals even crossed the Straights of Gibraltar and used North Africa as a staging ground to attack the city of Rome.

According to one legend, Romans abandoned the mainland to settle on the islands of the Venetian lagoons. By moving to the swampy islands, the Romans avoided a Hun invasion a few decades later. Over the next several centuries, people would continue to build up the islands of the lagoon until they became the majestic city of Venice.

450: HUMAN SETTLERS REACH MADAGASCAR

By the 5th century, large numbers of settlers had reached the island of Madagascar off the coast of Africa. While some evidence suggests that humans reached Madagascar thousands of years earlier, many scholars believe people first reached the island around 1,500 years ago.

When settlers reached Madagascar, they found an island populated by towering elephant birds, lemurs the size of men, pygmy hippos, and giant tortoises.

But where did the first settlers come from? Although Madagascar sits about 250 miles from the coast of Africa, one study suggested that the early settlers came from Indonesia. Over time, Madagascar became an important stopping point on Indian Ocean trade routes.

452: POPE LEO I MEETS WITH ATTILA TO CONVINCE HIM NOT TO ATTACK ROME.

In Rome, the pope eclipsed the emperor in 452. That year, as Attila and his Huns threatened to attack Rome, Pope Leo I intervened. He rode outside the city wall to meet with Attila. After their meeting, Attila and the Huns withdrew, sparing Rome.

What happened during the meeting between Pope Leo and Attila? No one knows what the pope said to convince Attila to turn back. A contemporary writer claimed Attila found the pope so impressive that he chose to spare Rome. A historian writing a few years later argued that Attila believed attacking the city might cause his own death. It's also possible that Leo offered Attila gold to withdraw.

Whatever convinced Attila, Pope Leo's actions protected Rome.

476: THE WESTERN ROMAN EMPIRE FALLS

The last Roman emperor in the city of Rome fell in 476. That year, Emperor Romulus Augustulus, a teenager named for Rome's founder and its first emperor, gave up his throne on September 4, 476. In his place, a Germanic leader named Odoacer crowned himself king.

Centuries later, scholars pointed to this moment as the fall of Rome. However, the Senate continued to meet in Rome and Germanic kings continued to style themselves after Roman emperors. In Constantinople, the capital of the Roman Empire, little changed. By 476, Rome's walls had fallen, the capital had lost control over its western territories, and

Rome didn't fall in a day—instead, it declined slowly over centuries until other empires eclipsed its power.

481: CLOVIS BECOMES KING OF THE FRANKS AND ESTABLISHES THE MEROVINGIAN DYNASTY.

Clovis was just 15 years old when he became King of the Franks. The ruler claimed his ancestors included a powerful sea dragon and named his dynasty the Merovingians. Success on the battlefield brought Clovis wealth and power. In a single year, Clovis captured Paris, Rouen, and Reims, and soon his tribe of Franks controlled much of Roman Gaul—giving it the modern name France.

The Frankish king also converted to Christianity. During a long battle, Clovis promised to convert if his forces won. After his victory, the king sent for priests to baptize him. The close alliance between Clovis and the church strengthened his position in France. The Merovingian dynasty would rule France for the next 200 years.

500S: THE MYTHICAL KINGS BEOWULF AND ARTHUR RULE.

Medieval English storytellers captivated audiences with tales of two noble rulers: Beowulf, king of the Geats, and Arthur of Camelot. While Beowulf fought against the monster Grendel, Arthur created the knights of the round table. According to legend, the kings both lived in the 6th century.

But were Beowulf and Arthur real? Little historical evidence remains about Beowulf, who reportedly ruled in Scandinavia. But some scholars believe Arthur defended Britain against Saxon invaders around the year 500. Most likely, the epic stories of Beowulf and Arthur blended fact and fiction, representing the qualities—bravery, loyalty, and strength—that medieval people most wanted in a ruler.

525: A MONK INVENTS THE ANNO DOMINI ERA CALENDAR.

In the 6th century, a monk named Dionysius Exiguus came up with a new calendar. He set year one at the birth of Jesus Christ and called his calendar *anno Domini*, or "in the year of the lord."

Why did Dionysius come up with a new calendar? In 525, the monk was writing an Easter table using the prior dating system. The older table counted from the rule of Emperor Diocletian, who had persecuted Christians. Rather than commemorate a pagan emperor, Dionysius proposed a new calendar.

Over the next several centuries, the anno domini calendar caught on, slowly replacing other dating systems that counted from the reign of Augustus or the creation of the world.

526: THE PHILOSOPHER BOETHIUS WRITES FROM JAIL

Boethius wrote his most important philosophical work from jail. In *Consolation of Philosophy*, Boethius lamented the world's harsh nature and inequality. But he eventually turned to a higher power that provided meaning in the world.

Why was an important Roman politician and philosopher writing from prison? In the 520s, Boethius took a position in the court of the Ostrogoth king Theoderic. During a falling out between Theoderic and the Byzantine empire, the king accused Boethius of treason and disloyalty.

Born as Rome's last western emperor fell, Boethius wanted to preserve classical knowledge by translating Aristotle and Plato into Latin. Although politics cost Boethius his life, his writings shaped philosophy for centuries.

527: JUSTINIAN BECOMES EMPEROR OF THE BYZANTINES

When Justinian became emperor in 527, he saw himself as a Roman. Although he governed from Constantinople, Justinian spoke Latin and followed Roman laws. As ruler, Justinian tried to retake all of Rome's lost territories, including in Africa and Italy. After decades of war, Justinian succeeded—but at a high price. His conquests nearly bankrupted the empire and left it vulnerable to invasion. And the land conquered by Justinian soon slipped away from his control.

While Justinian defined himself as Roman, today scholars see him as one of the most important Byzantine emperors. He created the legal code that ruled the Byzantines for centuries, built the Hagia Sophia church, and positioned himself as an important leader in the church.

548: THEODORA, AN INFLUENTIAL BYZANTINE EMPRESS, DIES

She rose from poverty to become one of the most powerful women in history. Theodora worked as a performer and actress before meeting Justinian. The law barred marriage between government officials and actresses, so Justinian changed the law. When he was crowned emperor, he insisted on Theodora holding the title empress and ruling as his equal.

Theodora advised Justinian on political strategies and signed her name to laws. She banned the trafficking of young girls, turned brothels into convents, and changed the empire's divorce laws to give women more rights. When Justinian faced a major revolt, Theodora encouraged him to die as a ruler rather than flee. After two decades transforming Constantinople and the Byzantine empire, Theodora died in 548.

550: IN MAHARASHTRA INDIA, THE CAVE-TEMPLE OF SHIVA IS BUILT.

Just a few miles from Mumbai on India's west coast, Elephanta Island hides an ancient secret. In the 6th century, the island's Hindu people carved massive, elaborate caves to honor the god Shiva. The cave temple, cut directly into the rocks, shows Shiva as a creator, preserver, and destroyer.

The caves, lined with pillars and connected through tunnels, cover the entire island, which became known as the village of caves. In all, the cave temple covers nearly 60,000 square feet, including a massive central chamber, courtyards, and smaller shrines. Hindu worshippers visited the temples for nearly a thousand years before Portuguese colonizers seized the island.

552: THE BYZANTINES BEGIN SILKWORM CULTIVATION

The Chinese held on to the secret of silk for centuries. But in 552, the Byzantines came up with a scheme to steal the secret. That year, two monks returned from a voyage to China. On their trip, they'd carefully observed how the Chinese raised silkworms and transformed their threads into silk.

In Constantinople, the monks sought out Emperor Justinian and offered to smuggle silkworms out of China—for a price. It took the monks two years to pull off the caper by hiding silkworm eggs inside hollow bamboo canes. Within a short time, the Byzantines set up silk factories throughout their empire. But just like the Chinese, the Byzantines kept the process secret so that Europeans didn't figure out how to make silk until the 13th century.

577: CHINA INVENTS MATCHES

As enemies laid siege to China's capital, the women of the court created a new invention. The military siege made it impossible to find tinder, leaving the city's people unable to start fires to cook food or heat their homes. In 577, the women in the capital came up with a solution: small sticks of wood coated in sulfur.

These were the first matches in history. Within a few centuries, matches were sold across China, often with the name "fire inch-sticks." The Chinese used matches to light their stoves and lamps. But matches also came in handy with another Chinese invention: fireworks.

595: POPE GREGORY SENDS MONKS TO ENGLAND

As Pope Gregory walked through a slave market in Rome, he saw sandy-haired young boys from England. The boys were "not Angles, but angels," Gregory remarked. The encounter inspired Pope Gregory to send monks to England to convert the pagans—and Celtic Christians–to Roman Christianity.

A wealthy Roman patrician, Gregory became pope in 590. "The towns are destroyed, the cities ruined, our fatherland is devastated," Gregory preached. "Where is the state of Rome, once the mistress of the world?" As pope, Gregory believed he could bring peace and stability to Europe. Rather than fight the Germanic invaders, he decided to convert them. His record of building up the church and sending out missions made Gregory a role model for later medieval popes.

607: IN JAPAN, PRINCE SHOTOKU FOUNDS THE HŌRYŪ-JI TEMPLE.

The world's oldest surviving wooden structure still stands in Japan. In 607, Prince Shotoku established the Hōryū-ji Temple to spread Buddhism throughout his country. The impressive temple complex included a main hall with its interior walls painted in bright colors to represent paradise. Nearby, a five-story wooden pagoda rises over 100 feet into the sky. Sculptures made from bronze and wood filled the temple.

Shotoku founded the temple as part of a larger project to modernize Japan. The prince also created a constitution, introduced a new calendar, and supported the arts. He also encouraged a closer relationship between Japan and China.

610: HERACLIUS CHANGES THE OFFICIAL LANGUAGE OF THE BYZANTINE EMPIRE.

For over a thousand years, Romans spoke Latin. But in 610, Emperor Heraclius officially changed the language of the eastern Roman Empire from Latin to Greek. By the 7th century, the change was largely symbolic—after Justinian, every emperor spoke Greek as his native language, and the empire's subjects largely spoke Greek.

Although emperors in Constantinople traced their rule back to Rome, the Byzantines evolved distinct practices. In the Byzantine empire, for example, the emperor became an almost holy figure. Byzantine rulers saw themselves as the head of the church and expected complete obedience. Rather than Augustus's model of "first among equals," visitors in the Byzantine court had to lay face-down on the floor to greet the emperor.

618: GAOZU FOUNDS THE TANG DYNASTY IN CHINA.

After generations of upheaval, the Tang dynasty brought a new golden age to China. Its first emperor, Gaozu, established a dynasty that ruled over China until the 10th century. Emperor for less than a decade, Gaozu established practices still used by the Chinese government today. He also created a legal code, reformed taxes to lighten the load on farmers, and built stronger relationships with neighbors like Korea, Japan, and Vietnam.

Trade flourished under the Tang, who conquered lands along the Silk Road to the Himalayas. The spread of printing increased literacy, while public libraries made books available to everyone. The Tang also saw advances in science, literature, and medicine that strengthened China's position as a world power.

622: MUHAMMAD MOVES FROM MECCA TO MEDINA

A merchant who crossed the desert by camel, Muhammad declared himself a prophet at the age of 40. In 610, the angel Gabriel visited Muhammad and commanded the merchant to spread the word of God.

But the polytheistic worshippers of Mecca rejected Muhammad's religious message. In 622, Muhammad and his followers moved from Mecca to Medina, where he ended a civil war and won more loyal followers.

In 630, Muhammad marched back to Mecca at the head of an army. The prophet soon united the entire Arabian Penninsula under Islam. Muhammad's move to Medina, known as the *hijrah*, marks the start of the Islamic calendar.

634: MUSLIM WARRIORS BEGIN EXPANDING INTO MESOPOTAMIA

Two years after the death of Muhammad, his followers left behind the desert sands of the Arabian Penninsula to conquer Persia, Egypt, and much of the Byzantine empire. These warriors soon created a cosmopolitan, diverse empire completely unlike the fragmented, nomadic peninsula that birthed them.

By the 8th century, the Islamic Caliphate stretched from Morocco and Spain in the west to the edges of India in the east. How did Muhammad's followers create such a massive empire so quickly? Many of the conquered territories were weak, and may non-Muslim people welcomed the caliphate.

In Byzantine territories, for example, religious persecutions left subjects happy to welcome Muslim rulers who embraced the "people of the book"—Jews and Christians. During the Ummayad Caliphate, which lasted from 661-750, only about 10% of the empire's subjects practiced Islam.

650: THE CHINESE USE PAPER MONEY FOR THE FIRST TIME.

Coins date back to around 600 BCE—and around 650 CE, paper bills first appeared in China. The earliest paper money wasn't issued by the government, though. Most were exchange notes or bills of credit handed out by banks or private lenders.

Soon, the government began using paper certificates to pay merchants in far-off corners of the empire. Rather than hauling coins to the Himalayas, they used paper bills. Merchants dubbed the bills "flying cash," because windy days sent them flying.

When Marco Polo returned from China with tales of paper bills, many Europeans found the idea unbelievable. Some even questioned whether Marco Polo had traveled to China at all.

660: THE FIRST QUR'AN IS FINISHED, COLLECTING MUHAMMAD'S SAYINGS FOR THE FAITHFUL.

A generation after Muhammad's death, his followers finished writing down the prophet's sayings. During Muhammad's lifetime, Muslims memorized his words, sometimes writing verses on leather, cloth, or paper. Other scribes etched words into stone.

In the years after Muhammad died, dozens of Muslims who had

memorized the Qur'an died in battle. Abu Bakr, the first caliph and the prophet's son-in-law, created a delegation of scribes to collect all of Muhammad's sayings in a book.

It took several decades to complete the process. The scribes had to present two witnesses for every single verse, and 33,000 Muslims then reviewed the text to make sure each word was correct. In total, the scribes recorded over 6,000 verses in the first Qur'an.

690: WU ZETIAN BECOMES EMPRESS OF CHINA

China's only empress came to power after plotting, seducing, and murdering her way to the throne. Empress Wu Zetian, whose name meant "ruler of heaven," started as an emperor's concubine before marrying his son and framing the emperor's first wife for murder.

Despite her backstabbing, Wu Zetian became a beloved ruler in China. She opened the civil service exam to all and ordered military commanders to take a competency exam. Empress Wu also instituted rewards for productive farmers, hired teachers for a public education system, and built irrigation systems. Under her rule, China expanded its borders and increased agricultural production.

Empress Wu earned many enemies among the aristocracy by redistributing their lands to farmers and raising their taxes. But by listening to the people—and even instituting a suggestion box—made Empress Wu popular with many in China.

THE AGE OF BUILDING (700-1100)

702: THE JAPANESE ESTABLISH THE TAIHO CODE.

Prince Shotoku sent Japanese students abroad to study in China during the 7th century. When those students returned, they encouraged Japan's rulers to adopt new laws and reform the bureaucracy. In 702, the Japanese borrowed from Tang dynasty laws to create the Taiho code.

The ambitious code divided Japan into provinces and districts, established a permanent capital, and centralized Japan's government. The state took over the training and administration of Buddhist monks while also enforcing a new legal code throughout the country. The Taiho code completed a century-long process of modernizing Japan and helped stabilize the country, which ushered in a golden age.

708: TEA BECOMES A POPULAR DRINK IN CHINA.

An ancient Chinese deity discovered tea while resting under a Camellia tree, according to legend. As he boiled water to drink, dried leaves from the tree landed in the pot and created tea. But for centuries, the Chinese mainly used tea in rituals or for medicinal purposes. Some ate tea leaves raw.

In the 8th century, tea became a popular drink throughout China. One explanation points to Buddhist monks, who relied on tea to stay awake during hours of meditation. As a result, monasteries often grew their own tea. Lu Yu, who studied at a monastery, wrote a popular book about tea in the 8th century that explained how to prepare and drink tea.

711: TARIQ IBN ZIYAD BURNS HIS BOATS AND SAILS THE STRAITS OF GIBRALTAR.

"Oh my warriors, whither would you flee?" commander Tariq ibn Ziyad told his army as they landed on the shores of Spain. "Behind you is the sea, before you, the enemy. You have left now only the hope of your courage and your constancy."

Outnumbered ten to one by Spanish forces, Tariq burned the ships his men used to cross the Straits of Gibraltar. With their only escape route gone, Tariq's army would either win or die trying.

After a fierce battle, Tariq's army won and took the Iberian Peninsula for the Umayyad Caliphate. The stunning victory ushered in eight centuries of Muslim rule in Iberia.

731: BEDE COMPLETES HIS HISTORY OF THE ENGLISH PEOPLE.

The history of the English people began with Julius Caesar's invasion, according to Bede. In his centuries-long account of England's conversion to Christianity, Bede began and ended with Rome. While Caesar brought Roman rule to Britain, Pope Gregory brought Christianity—also from Rome.

Bede entered a monastery at seven years old and spent the rest of his life reading and writing about religion. His writings became the authoritative account of early English history and the relationships between kings and the church. Looking back at his life, Bede wrote, "It has ever been my delight to learn or to teach or to write."

750: ARABIAN MATHEMATICIANS ADOPT NUMBERS DEVELOPED IN INDIA.

While the Romans chiseled their long, unwieldy numbers into stone, Indian mathematicians developed a new number system. Unlike the more complicated Roman numerals, based on earlier tally lines, this new system created nine different symbols to represent the numbers one through nine.

The simpler counting system soon moved from India to North Africa, where Arabian mathematicians slowly transformed Indian numerals into our modern Arabic numerals.

For centuries, Europeans recorded the years and counted money using Roman numerals—until an Italian mathematician named Leonardo Fibonacci visited Algeria around 1200. There, Fibonacci learned "the art of the Indians' nine symbols," which he promoted in Europe.

800: CHARLEMAGNE BECOMES THE FIRST HOLY ROMAN EMPEROR.

In 800, the king of the Franks visited Rome so the pope could crown him emperor. Charlemagne had conquered much of Western Europe and created the mightiest empire since the Romans, but he lacked one thing: an emperor's crown. So on Christmas day, Charlemagne declared himself the first Holy Roman Emperor.

Charlemagne created a united Christian Europe by forcing conquered Germanic tribes to convert at swordpoint. Under his rule, the Carolingian Renaissance spread culture and scholarship across Europe. But when he took the title emperor, Charlemagne angered the Byzantine rulers in Constantinople who saw themselves as the true Roman emperors.

For centuries after his death, Europeans held up Charlemagne as the model of a Christian king—and claimed he would someday return from sleeping under a mountain to revive his empire.

801: JIA DAN PRESENTS A MAP OF CHINA TO THE EMPEROR.

In 801, a geographer named Jia Dan drew a map of China. Creating the map took nearly two centuries, as Jia Dan interviewed visitors from foreign lands and spoke with merchants to learn more about geography. His final map measured more than 30 feet across, listing hundreds of place names, trading centers, and administrative divisions.

Jia Dan's work went far beyond drawing China's borders. He also described land and sea trade routes, wrote a history of the Great Wall, and described Arab ports and trade goods. The geographer's map became an important source of knowledge for generations, though unfortunately, the original map does not survive.

813: THE ABBASID CALIPH IN BAGHDAD COLLECTS ANCIENT GREEK TEXTS.

In 750, the Abbasid Caliphate rose to power and moved the capital of the Islamic empire from Damascus to Baghdad. Abbasid Caliphs modeled their empire on the Persians—the son of one caliph even said, "The Persians ruled for a thousand years and did not need us Arabs even for a day. We have been ruling them for one or two centuries and cannot do without them for an hour."

From the beginning, the Abbasids looked to outside cultures for knowledge and inspiration. As the Qur'an taught, "the ink of a scholar is more holy than the blood of a martyr." During the Islamic Golden Age, caliphs collected manuscripts from around the world. In 813, one ruler sent scholars to Constantinople to collect scientific writings from ancient Greece. This effort to collect knowledge from around the world led the Abbasids to create the House of Wisdom.

830: THE ABBASIDS CREATE THE HOUSE OF WISDOM.

As champions of knowledge, the Abbasids founded a library to collect the most important texts from the classical period through the 9th century. Known as the House of Wisdom, the library preserved the writings of Plato, Aristotle, Euclid, and other Greek writers. Many of these texts might have been lost completely without Abbasid help.

The House of Wisdom was more than a library. It was also a translation center. Scholars would collect works from ancient Greece, Persia, and India. Then they would translate the manuscripts into Arabic. Scholars also traveled the world looking for important texts. By bringing together the wisdom of the world, the Abbasids fueled their scientific advances, breaking new ground in mathematics, medicine, astronomy, and other fields.

850: THE FRANKS DEVELOP THE THREE-FIELD SYSTEM.

The Romans relied on slave labor in the fields. But the Franks relied on horses. In the 9th century, French farmers developed three innovations that transformed agriculture. First, they created a bronze horseshoe that helped horses plow through the heavy soil in France. Second, they invented a horse collar that gave horses more pulling power.

Finally, the Franks developed a new crop rotation. Rather than rotating between two fields, leaving half of the land fallow, farmers moved to a three-field system. Farmers harvested wheat and rye in the fall while growing crops like peas, beans, oats, and barley in the spring, leaving the third field fallow. The system kept the soil rich and fertilized, increasing agricultural yields by 33%.

868: CHINA CREATES THE FIRST KNOWN PRINTED BOOK, THE DIAMOND SUTRA.

On the 13th day of the 4th moon of the 9th year of Xianton—or May 11, 868—Wang Jie printed the oldest known book. Called the Diamond Sutra, the book reproduced a Buddhist text "for universal free distribution by Wang Jie on behalf of his two parents."

The Diamond Sutra was lost for centuries until a monk discovered a copy in a former Silk Road trading post in the Gobi Desert. Apparently, someone hid over 40,000 scrolls in a cave back in 1000 CE, including the Diamond Sutra.

The text included the Buddha's advice on the world: "So you should view this fleeting world—a star at dawn, a bubble in a stream, a flash of lightning in a summer cloud, a flickering lamp, a phantom, and a dream."

900: FIREWORKS FIRST APPEAR IN CHINA THANKS TO THE INVENTION OF GUNPOWDER.

Thousands of years ago, the Chinese created a natural "firecracker" when they discovered that tossing bamboo stalks into fire created a loud bang. But around 900, the Chinese created the first fireworks by combining the ancient bamboo firecracker with gunpowder.

During the Tang dynasty, a Chinese chemist combined potassium nitrate, charcoal, and sulfur to create gunpowder. By filling a stalk of bamboo with gunpowder, the Chinese invented fireworks. Over time, firework makers began using paper tubes instead of bamboo. Unlike modern fireworks, these early examples didn't come in fancy colors.

Instead, they created a loud bang and sparkling lights that were supposed to frighten the spirits away.

935: TAEJO CHANGES THE NAME OF HIS KINGDOM TO KORYO--KOREA.

In 918, Taejo established a new kingdom in Korea and named it Goryeo or Koryo. The name, which means "high and beautiful" evolved into the word Korea. After a period of decline and instability, Taejo ushered in a period of growth in Korea. He built schools, lowered taxes on farmers, and traded with nearby powers like China.

Taejo also created a list of rules for Korea's rulers, which must be "read morning and night and forever used as a mirror of reflection." The rules encouraged leaders to uphold traditions, act fairly, and follow the motto "no complacency." Taejo's successors ruled in Korea until nearly the 15th century.

950: WOMEN IN A CHINESE HAREM INVENT PLAYING CARDS.

Women in the imperial harem had a lot of free time. Around 950, a group of Chinese women invented the first playing cards. Made from printed sheets of paper, playing cards entertained the women so much that they soon became popular outside of the harem.

According to one source, an emperor celebrated New Year's Eve by playing "the game of leaves" with his ministers. Scholar-officials pulled out cards to play games during banquets. And soon cards spread across Asia.

Playing cards reached Europe by the 14th century, with some changes. Instead of the Chinese suit of coins, Europeans played with four suits representing swords, cups, staves, and coins.

950: EUROPEANS STUDY MEDICINE AT A MEDICAL SCHOOL IN SALERNO, ITALY.

In Salerno, physicians studied ancient Greek medical texts to learn how to treat human illnesses. Positioned at the southern tip of Italy, Salerno became a crossroads for Mediterranean knowledge. The medical school taught Arabic medical texts that translated Greek writings.

Unlike later colleges, Salerno welcomed both men and women to study medicine, anatomy, and surgery. As the school's reputation grew, patients traveled across Europe for treatments.

The close connection between Salerno and Sicily helped spread knowledge. Once a Byzantine territory, Muslim Moors conquered Sicily in the 9th century. As a result, it became an important interchange between Greek, Arab, and European knowledge.

981: ERIK THE RED SAILS TO GREENLAND AFTER HE IS EXILED FROM ICELAND.

At just ten years old, Erik the Red left Norway with his father, who'd been accused of manslaughter. A few decades later, after settling in Iceland, Erik was also exiled for manslaughter. Once again, Erik the Red sailed west. After crossing over 1,000 miles of arctic waters, he reached Greeland.

Erik explored Greenland, naming fjords and rivers after himself. Although he found rough terrain, Erik named the new territory Greenland, hoping to encourage other Vikings to join him. Within a few years, Erik had brought hundreds of Vikings to establish colonies on Greenland, which soon grew into the thousands. The Viking settlements on Greenland lasted for centuries, dying out around the time Columbus sailed to the New World.

1001: VIKINGS ESTABLISH SETTLEMENTS IN NORTH AMERICA

After Erik the Red created a permanent Viking settlement in Greenland, his son continued the family tradition of sailing westward. Leif Erikson heard stories of land to the west from a Viking who'd been blown off course by a storm. Around 1001, Erikson crossed the Labrador Sea with thirty men and landed in Newfoundland—the first Europeans to reach the New World nearly five centuries before Columbus.

The Vikings established a settlement called Vinland, or the land of wine, after the local berries they fermented. The Vikings returned to the new continent to collect timber and trade with local people. But unlike Greenland, where Vikings lived for centuries, the Norse settlements in North America were temporary.

1001: IN JAPAN, MURASAKI SHIKIBU WRITES THE TALE OF GENJI, THE FIRST NOVEL IN HISTORY.

Murasaki Shikibu lived in Japan's imperial capital as a court lady. After carefully observing palace intrigues and the dance of etiquette, Murasaki wrote The Tale of Genji, considered the first novel in history.

In the novel, Prince Genji navigates the court. In his youth, the prince builds relationships, falls in love, and struggles with heartbreak. As an adult, the prince battles his way back from exile and raises the child born from his wife's affair.

The Tale of Genji captures life at the imperial court and reveals the important roles women played in government. As Murasaki wrote, "There are as many sorts of women as there are women."

1014: PERSIAN SCHOLAR AVICENNA WRITES THE BOOK OF HEALING.

Born in a small village in Persia, Avicenna read the entire works of Aristotle as a teenager. As an adult, Avicenna became one of the most influential writers of the pre-modern era. In over 450 works, Avicenna wrote on astronomy, geography, mathematics, and physics. He synthesized and built on ancient Greek, Persian, and Indian works as the greatest thinker of the Islamic Golden Age.

Avicenna's most famous work, *The Book of Healing*, explained how mountains formed, developed a theory of motion, and laid out a scientific method of inquiry. Physicians across Europe and the Islamic world turned to Avicenna's medical writings for centuries.

Speaking of his own accomplishments, Avicenna wrote in verse, "From the depth of the black earth up to Saturn's apogee, All the problems of the universe have been solved by me."

1054: ASTRONOMERS AROUND THE WORLD OBSERVE A SUPERNOVA.

On July 4, 1054, Chinese astronomers recorded an unusual sight in the sky. A new star appeared, and at first, it was so bright that people around the world could see it during the day. The star remained visible at night for nearly two years before it vanished.

It wasn't the first time Chinese astronomers saw "guest stars"—or what we now call supernovas. Between 532 BCE-1064 CE, the Chinese tracked 75 supernovas.

Thousands of miles away, Arabic astronomers also wrote about the supernova, and in North America, Native Americans tracked its appearance.

Today we know that the "guest star" was the supernova that created the Crab Nebula.

1066: WILLIAM THE CONQUEROR CROSSES THE ENGLISH CHANNEL TO BECOME KING.

In 1066, Harold Godwinson crowned himself king of England. But his throne wasn't secure. First, Norway's king, Harald Hardrada, invaded and tried to seize control. After fighting off the Norwegians, Harold

Godwinson marched south to face an invasion by William, the Duke of Normandy.

But Godwinson's luck didn't hold twice. In the Battle of Hastings, William the Conqueror emerged victorious and crowned himself King William I at Westminster Abbey.

William the Conqueror and his Norman Conquest would shape Britain for a thousand years. As king, William handed out land to Norman aristocrats and founded new cathedrals across the country. The Normans turned French into the ruling language of England for centuries and created a close relationship between England and France.

1080: THE MATHEMATICIAN AND ASTRONOMER OMAR KHAYYÁM WRITES POETRY.

"Be happy for this moment," wrote Omar Khayyám. "This moment is your life." An accomplished mathematician and astronomer born in Persia, Khayyám mixed his scientific pursuits with poetry.

In 1073, Khayyám visited Isfahan, the capital of the Seljuk Empire, where the sultan asked him to create the most accurate calendar ever made. In Isfahan, Khayyám created an observatory to track Saturn's movements for 30 years. Drawing on his astronomical observations, Khayyám created history's most accurate calculation of the length of a year.

While he calculated and studied the skies, Khayyám also wrote poetry. His *Rubáiyát*, written in a traditional Persian style, earned him the title "astronomer-poet of Persia."

1080: THE BAYEUX TAPESTRY TELLS THE STORY OF THE NORMAN CONQUEST.

William the Conqueror wanted the world to remember his deeds. And the Bayeux tapestry cataloged his victory at the Battle of Hastings. Created over a 15-year period, the Bayeux tapestry weaves nearly 60 scenes of the Normans conquering England. Surrounded by horses, ships, and dogs, William's loyal warriors cross the English Channel and confront their rivals.

In one scene, the Normans build ships for their invasion, gathering up supplies including a barrel of wine. During the Battle of Hastings, the Norman riders crush the Anglo-Saxons with their superior weapons. The tapestry even captures the battlefield deaths.

The Bayeux tapestry does more than chronicle the battles. It captures daily life in the 11th century in vivid colors.

1086: THE DOMESDAY BOOK CREATES A CENSUS OF ENGLAND.

After conquering England, King William turned his attention to ruling his new territory. In 1086, the king requested a survey of his lands. The Domesday Book recorded every landowner in England, their property, and each tenant and serf. The detailed census provided key information for England's new ruler.

William used the Domesday Book to govern more effectively. The census helped the king levy new taxes and require feudal service from his vassals. In fact, the threat of a Danish invasion the year before may have encouraged William to order the survey.

Today, the Domesday Book resides in the National Archives, where scholars rely on it to understand medieval England.

1094: SU SONG BUILDS AN ASTRONOMICAL CLOCK TOWER IN KAIFENG, CHINA.

Like his 11th century Persian contemporaries Avicenna and Omar Khayyám, Su Song blended art and science. An astronomer, mathematician, and cartographer, Su Song also wrote poetry and collected art.

In 1094, Su Song built a massive astronomical clock in China's capital, Kaifeng. The clock used water to calculate time. An 11-foot wheel lined with 36 scoops would move as water poured in at a constant rate. The wheel's turning drove a bronze star chart and armillary sphere. As Su Song explained, "The heavens move without ceasing but so also does water flow."

Unfortunately, the Manchurians took the clock apart in 1127 to move it to Beijing—but they couldn't figure out how to put it back together.

1096: THE UNIVERSITY OF OXFORD IN ENGLAND HOLDS ITS FIRST LECTURES.

The University of Oxford predates every other university in the English-speaking world. In 1096, scholars in Oxford held their first lectures. But the university didn't take off until the mid-12th century.

By that time, many English students crossed the channel to attend the University of Paris. But in 1167, King Henry II banned his subjects from enrolling at the rival university. In response, many returned to Oxford and helped transform the city into a center of higher education. Scholars from the continent traveled to Oxford to lecture students, who flocked to the area.

In the 13th century, Oxford established its first residence halls and colleges. University College, Balliol, and Merton College, which date to the mid-13th century, represent the university's oldest colleges.

1101: TRADERS FIRST ESTABLISH TIMBUKTU IN WESTERN AFRICA.

Timbuktu became one of the richest cities in the world under the Mali Empire. In 1101, nomadic traders founded the city as a seasonal camp. They named the city after a woman left behind to watch over the camp while the nomads traveled the Sahara Desert.

Within centuries, Timbuktu had grown as a key trading center. Travelers who carried gold and salt across the Sahara stopped in Timbuktu, and after converting to Islam, rulers build mosques in the city and transformed it into a center of Islamic study. By 1450, the population of Timbuktu stood at 100,000—with scholars making up one in four inhabitants.

1102: EPIC POEMS CELEBRATE CHARLEMAGNE AS THE PERFECT KING.

The epic poetry of the 12th century held up Charlemagne as the ideal feudal king. These so-called *chansons* told the stories of kings and legends from the past. Originally set to music, traveling *jongleurs* would spread stories around France and other parts of Europe.

The most famous of these epic poems was the *Song of Roland*. A tale of Charlemagne's army battling Muslim invaders, the poem promoted religious warfare in the age of the Crusades. It also offered a code of honor for knights and warned of the dangers of breaking the code.

The world of noble knights and just kings depicted in medieval poems were more an ideal than the reality. But they gave men and women role models to imitate in 12th century Europe.

1104: VENICE FOUNDS THE ARSENAL TO BUILD SHIPS.

At its height, Venice's Arsenal could build a ship per day. Founded in 1104, the Arsenal used an assembly line process to build ships. As many as 16,000 workers built military and merchant ships at the Arsenal.

The Venetians innovated when it came to ships. They cut parts to size, speeding up the assembly process. They also ordered ropemakers to add a unique combination of colored strands to their ropes. If a rope broke, the Venetians could easily know which ropemaker to blame.

Thanks to the Arsenal, Venice created a military fleet that dominated the Mediterranean for centuries. With outposts throughout the eastern Mediterranean, the Venetians played a central role in transporting luxury goods from the East to Europe.

1120: THE TROUBADOURS OF PROVENCE DEVELOP A NEW FORM OF POETRY.

In southern France, medieval troubadours began singing about chivalry and courtly love in the 12th century. The first troubadours traveled from village to village near Provence, reciting poems written in Occitan to eager audiences.

In their romantic poems, the troubadours would tell the tale of Lancelot and Guinevere, the noble Knights of the Round Table, and King Arthur's Camelot. In their songs, the troubadours linked the code of chivalry with romantic love.

Soon, royals fought to hire the best troubadours to entertain their courts while nobles invited troubadours to their estates. The troubadours even joined Crusaders on their journeys to the Holy Land where they recorded the deeds of knights.

1137: THE HEIR TO THE FRENCH THRONE MARRIES ELEANOR, THE DUCHESS OF AQUITAINE.

At just 15 years old, Eleanor of Aquitaine inherited an enormous territory on France's Atlantic coast. Eleanor became the only woman in history who was both queen of France and queen of England.

Just months after marrying the heir to the French throne in 1137, Eleanor and her husband were crowned king and queen. But the marriage fell apart and after an annulment, Eleanor married the Duke of Normandy—who became King of England two years later.

Eleanor angered her royal husband by supporting their son's usurpation of the throne—which landed the queen in prison. Later, she ruled as a regent for her son Richard the Lionhearted. Not only did Eleanor shape English politics, but she also supported the arts and encouraged courtly love and chivalry.

1150: THE UNIVERSITY OF PARIS IS FOUNDED

When the University of Paris began holding lectures in the 12th century, students could study four fields: the liberal arts, medicine, law, and theology. The liberal arts provided foundational training in logic, grammar, mathematics, and astronomy, preparing students to join one of the advanced fields.

Professors at the university had to pass an examination to demonstrate their expertise and earn an appointment from the head of the school. Students would then arrange to take courses from the faculty.

Students from across Europe flocked to the university, which divided its students by region: France, Normandy, Picard, England, and German. Along with the University of Bologna, the University of Paris created an influential model for later universities.

1150: A FEMALE DOCTOR IN SALERNO NAMED TROTA WRITES THE TROTULA.

In Europe's medical capital, Trota wrote one of the most influential medical texts in medieval Europe in the 12th century. Her book, which focused on women's medicine, was called the *Trotula*. The text included medical treatments for multiple conditions, including cures tested in Salerno.

The *Trotula* drew on ancient texts by Galen and Greek physicians that reached Salerno from the Islamic world. But the text also included wisdom from Trota's own medical experience. She recommended giving women opiates during labor, even though that contradicted the Christian belief that God wanted women to suffer in childbirth because of Eve's sin.

Trota's medical writings were translated into a dozen languages and shaped women's medicine for centuries.

1152: FREDERICK BARBAROSSA RULES GERMANY AND ITALY

Frederick Barbarossa ruled as one of the most powerful medieval Holy Roman Emperors. In 1152, the Germans elected him king, and three years later the Italians also named him king. Thanks to a treaty with the pope, Frederick also became Holy Roman Emperor.

As emperor, Frederick ruled over a divided territory made up of independent city-states. He spent much of his life marching armies from Germany to Italy to put down rebellions against his rule. In his later years, Frederick coordinated with King Richard I of England and King Philip II of France to go on a crusade. But as Barbarossa's army marched to the Holy Land, he fell off his horse and drowned in a river.

1163: IN PARIS, CONSTRUCTION BEGINS ON NOTRE DAME.

King Louis VII laid the cornerstone piece of Notre Dame cathedral in 1163. Located on the Ile de la Cite, an island in the Seine, the cathedral would welcome kings, popes, and hunchbacks for eight centuries.

It took nearly 200 years to build Notre Dame. The French carried stones up the Seine for decades to build their massive Gothic cathedral. When construction began, European architects had not yet developed the flying buttress. But in the 13th century, the builders added flying buttresses, which let them make higher, thinner walls with more stained glass windows.

When the cathedral was finally complete in 1345, it stood as an example of the French Gothic style of architecture. The cathedral's rose windows, towering vault, and powerful bells made Notre Dame a historic landmark.

1176: CONSTRUCTION BEGINS ON LONDON BRIDGE

The Romans built the city of London on the River Thames around 50 CE. But for a thousand years, travelers had to cross the bridge by ferry or a dangerous wooden bridge. In 1176, King Henry II ordered a permanent stone bridge after multiple fires destroyed the wooden bridges.

London Bridge was more than a river crossing. It also housed buildings that stretched up to seven stories, a drawbridge, and waterwheels. Horse-drawn carts, herds of cattle, and Londoners crossed the bridge every day. And the children's rhyme about London Bridge was based on a true story—the bridge collapsed several times between the 13th-15th centuries.

1179: HILDEGARD OF BINGEN CREATES SCIENTIFIC AND MEDICAL WRITINGS.

From her convent in Germany, a 12th-century nun wrote about science and medicine. Hildegard of Bingen built on the ancient Greek concept that healthy bodies had balanced humors, while an imbalance within the body could cause disease. The nun proposed treatments including a healthy diet and herbal remedies to keep the body in balance.

But Hildegard also linked health with spirituality. As a Christian mystic, Hildegard argued that health also required a virtuous soul.

Although the Catholic Church limited the role of women in religion, Hildegard pushed the boundaries. She gave sermons to men and proclaimed her authority in philosophy, medicine, and natural history. Hildegard also wrote the only medieval musical that still exists.

1180: IN CORDOBA, AVERROËS WRITES INFLUENTIAL COMMENTARIES ON ARISTOTLE.

Cordoba, Spain served as the intellectual capital of Europe for centuries, thanks to tolerant Muslim caliphs who supported Jewish and

Muslim scholars. One of these scholars was Averroës, who worked in the court of Cordoba as a philosopher.

Averroës wrote influential commentaries on Aristotle and Plato while also working as a judge. These commentaries, which included summaries and extensive critiques, shaped how later scholars read classical Greek texts. Every commentary Averroës wrote on Aristotle was translated into Latin and included in copies of Aristotle's complete works. Averroës, who wrote in Arabic, also saw his work translated into Hebrew.

Averroës spoke to the 12th-century interest in logic by claiming "truth does not contradict truth."

1180: WINDMILLS BECOME COMMON IN FLANDERS AND THE NETHERLANDS.

In Babylonia, Hammurabi vowed to create windmills to irrigate the fields. But it took centuries for engineers to harness the power of the wind. Ancient Greek engineers created a wind-powered organ, while Tibetan monks created prayer wheels powered by wind.

Medieval Persians developed vertical windmills to pump water and grind grain. Soon, their innovation spread to China and Europe. By the 12th century, Flanders and the Netherlands had created entire industries around their windmills. Low-lying countries relied on windmills to pump water out of wetlands and swamps, transforming them into arable land. In Holland, people used windmills and seawalls to improve living conditions and limit flooding.

1185: IN INDIA, BHASKARA INVENTS DIFFERENTIAL CALCULUS

At India's astronomical observatory, Bhaskara watched the sky. Using complex mathematical calculations, he determined the exact time it takes for the Earth to circle the sun. Bhaskara's calculation was within 4 minutes of modern calculations.

As one of the best mathematicians in the world, Bhaskara solved unsolvable equations, introduced decimals, and invented differential calculus 500 years before Newton and Leibniz battled over the concept.

The mathematician also observed the planets, recorded eclipses, and designed new mathematical techniques to understand the stars. Outside of his scientific work, he was devoted to his family. Bhaskara named his first book after his daughter.

1191: TEA FROM CHINA BECOMES POPULAR IN JAPAN.

The medieval Japanese carefully studied their neighbors in China. Japanese priests visited China to learn more about Buddhism and Chinese culture. On one visit, the priests brought back tea. Initially popular among Buddhist monks, tea quickly became a royal drink when a 9th-century emperor tried to plant his own tea.

In the 12th century, tea became even more popular after a Zen monk named Eisai brought back tea seeds to Japan's southernmost island. Now, tea was more than a royal drink—it became accessible to nearly everyone, as Eisai's tea seeds spread across the country. Even the samurai class turned to tea as a hangover remedy.

In 1211, Eisai wrote Japan's first book on tea, recommending the drink for health reasons. "Tea is the most wonderful medicine for nourishing one's health," Eisai proclaimed. "It is the secret of long life."

THE MEDIEVAL WORLD (1200-1300)

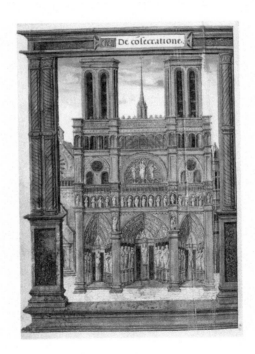

1202: LEONARDO FIBONACCI DEVELOPS THE FIBONACCI SEQUENCE.

After traveling in North Africa, Italian Leonardo Fibonacci realized that Europeans lagged far behind in mathematics. Thanks in part to contact with India, the Islamic World used Arabic numbers and

In 1202, Leonardo Fibonacci published *Liber Abaci* or *The Book of Calculations*. The influential book told Europe's tradesmen how to use math in their business. He showed how to use Arabic arithmetic to track profits, calculate interest,

Fibonacci also introduced a sequence of numbers sometimes called "nature's secret code." The Fibonacci sequence (0, 1, 1, 2, 3, 5, 8, 13, 21, etc.) can be used to understand the curve of a seashell and the dimensions of the Great Pyramid of Giza. But Fibonacci didn't come up with the sequence—it was another insight that came via Sanskrit and Arabic texts.

1206: GENGHIS KHAN BECOMES THE GREAT KHAN OF THE MONGOLS.

At nine years old, Genghis Khan watched his father's murder and saw his family exiled in the harsh Mongolian Steppes. But as an adult, Genghis Khan would bring together the divided Mongol tribes and become their leader.

Before he could conquer a third of the known world, Genghis Khan had to unite the warring Mongol tribes. He succeeded by blending diplomacy and ruthlessness. After beating a rival on the battlefield, Genghis Khan would absorb their fighters into his growing army. He took wives from rival tribes to band the Mongols together. And he showed them the benefits of unifying.

In 1206, the Mongol clans met and chose Genghis Khan to rule them. Over the next two decades, the Mongols would conquer nearly all of the Asian continent, including powerful countries like China.

1215: KING JOHN OF ENGLAND SIGNS THE MAGNA CARTA.

King John was one of England's least popular kings. After taxing his barons relentlessly to fund unsuccessful overseas wars, England's barons revolted. They forced the king to sign the Magna Carta, a charter that restricted the monarch's powers, to prevent a civil war.

The Magna Carta served as a contract between a feudal ruler and his vassals. By promising not to imprison people without trial and limiting the king's power to tax, the Magna Carta governed how the king ruled. As Europe's first written constitution, the Magna Carta inspired the American Founding Fathers.

It also established the idea that rulers had an obligation to treat their subjects fairly. While the Magna Carta mainly focuses on the relationship between the king and nobility, it encapsulates the concept of a ruler's responsibilities to their people.

1220: THE CHARTRES CATHEDRAL INSTALLS STAINED GLASS WINDOWS.

Starting in the 12th century, Europeans decorated their churches with elaborate stained glass windows. By heating sand and wood ash, glass-makers would create a blank canvas to color with powdered metals. When the liquid glass cooled,

The stained glass windows in the Chartres Cathedral, installed around 1220, remain the most complete from the medieval era. They tell the story of the Virgin Mary, France's kings, and the saints. The three rose windows warn visitors about the Last Judgement.

After a fire nearly destroyed the cathedral in 1194, the people of Chartres rebuilt their church, adding in the stained glass windows. Today, more than 150 stained glass windows survive from the early 13th century.

1250: FREDERICK II, THE HOLY ROMAN EMPEROR, DIES.

From his court in Palermo, Sicily, Frederick II ruled over most of Italy and Germany as the Holy Roman Emperor. Fluent in six languages, including Arabic, Frederick clashed with popes who feared his power would eclipse their own.

In 1227, Pope Gregory IX excommunicated Frederick, casting him out of the church. But while excommunicated, the Holy Roman Emperor sailed to the Holy Land where he negotiated a treaty that put Jerusalem back in the hands of the Crusaders without bloodshed. The truce earned Frederick another title: King of Jerusalem.

Frederick became a model for medieval kings. He hired scholars to translate Greek and Arabic works at his court, wrote the first treatise on falconry, and boasted a menagerie of giraffes, exotic birds, and cheetahs.

1250: THE ANNUAL HORSE RACE IN SIENA KNOWN AS THE PALIO BEGINS.

The hillside Tuscan town of Siena held public games in its large central piazza. Men met to box or joust, while Siena imported bulls for fights in the 16th century. But the most spectacular races were known as the Palio.

A horse race that pitted the city's districts against each other, the Palio sent ten horses racing around the outer ring of the piazza. Run twice a year, the Palio gave one district bragging rights until the next race.

The Palio continues today. Twice a summer, 50,000 people crowd into the piazza to watch jockeys fly across the dirt-covered piazza without saddles.

1267: ROGER BACON WRITES THE OPUS MAJUS

"The things of this world cannot be made known without a knowledge of mathematics," Roger Bacon proclaimed in his *Opus Majus*.

A nearly 900-page work, the book collected everything Bacon knew about mathematics, language, technology, and optics. In between proposing flying machines, Bacon described how to make gunpowder and proposed an experimental method for science.

Bacon promoted teaching the sciences in universities and taught at Oxford. But he ran into trouble with the Catholic Church after criticizing corruption and calling out greedy priests. As a result, Bacon spent time in prison for heresy.

1275: THE ANASAZI LEAVE THEIR CLIFF HOUSES

For centuries, the Anasazi built cliff dwellings in the American Southwest. Carved into the sides of sandstone canyons, entire villages thrived. At Chaco Canyon, for example, buildings stretched five stories high and housed thousands. At Mesa Verde, the Cliff Palace served as a ceremonial center for the region.

The ancestors of the Pueblo people, the Anasazi built their elaborate cliff dwellings to defend their communities against enemies. But in the late 13th century, the Anasazi abandoned their cliff dwellings, leaving behind a mystery for archaeologists. One theory points to a climate crisis. A decades-long drought made the Southwest uninhabitable. Yet the Anasazi had weathered previous droughts. Another theory blames warfare that even cliff dwellers could not escape.

Whatever drove the Anasazi from their homes, they left behind a stunning reminder of their ingenuity.

1280: VENETIANS INVENT THE FIRST EYEGLASSES

The Venetians were master glassblowers in the 13th century. They outfitted castles and palaces across Europe with their glass. But the Venetians also used glass for other purposes. Around 1280, the Venetians invented the first eyeglasses. Made from two small lenses that rested in metal frames, the glasses helped people see.

It took over a hundred years before eyeglasses were popular enough to appear in art. In 1352, Tommaso da Modena painted an image of monks creating manuscripts, and one wore glasses.

Before 1280, the Venetians had sold "reading stones," or medieval magnifying lenses. Readers could set the glass on a book to magnify the text. But the smaller, more portable eyeglasses soon became more popular than reading stones.

1281: A POWERFUL STORM STOPS THE MONGOLS FROM INVADING JAPAN FOR A SECOND TIME.

It was a divine wind—a *kamikaze*—that saved Japan in 1281. That year, the Mongols invaded the islands of Japan with 4,400 ships carrying 100,000 men. Led by Kublai Khan, who had already conquered China and Korea, the Mongol invaders planned to add Japan to their empire.

But after landing in Japan, a typhoon struck the Mongol fleet, sinking many of their ships. More than half of the Mongol force was killed, forcing Kublai Khan to withdraw his army.

The Japanese called the storm a *kamikaze* or divine wind since it saved Japan from invasion. Ironically, a typhoon also destroyed an earlier and much smaller Mongol force that tried to invade a decade earlier.

1295: MARCO POLO RETURNS TO VENICE FROM CHINA.

At just 17 years old, Marco Polo left Venice behind to travel the Silk Road. On a journey that lasted 24 years, Polo saw the Gobi desert, the majestic court of Kublai Khan, and the riches of the east.

When Marco Polo returned to Venice in 1295, he barely spoke

Venetian and no one recognized him. His stories of the Silk Road and China might have been lost forever if Polo hadn't become a prisoner of war. While commanding a Venetian ship against the Genoese, Polo was captured and thrown into prison. He began telling stories of his travels to another prisoner, who wrote them down.

Tales of China's fabulous wealth were almost too much for Europeans to believe—and many concluded that Marco Polo made up the entire story. But today, most scholars agree that Polo traveled to China.

1297: WILLIAM WALLACE ATTACKS THE ENGLISH IN THE FIGHT FOR SCOTTISH INDEPENDENCE.

In 1297, William Wallace rode into battle against the English. A knight with powerful Scottish allies, Wallace played a central role in the fight for Scottish independence.

During the Battle of Stirling Bridge, Wallace handily defeated the English by outmaneuvering the larger enemy force. But the next year, the English returned and bested Wallace. A hunted man, Wallace evaded the English until 1305, when they captured and executed him.

The Scots saw Wallace as a martyr in their fight for freedom. His death motivated fellow Scotsmen like Robert the Bruce to continue the fight for independence. Wallace also became a national hero for the Scots.

1300: GOTHIC CATHEDRALS BEGIN USING FLYING BUTTRESSES

The massive stone cathedrals built across Europe in the medieval period weighed tons – literally. But a new architectural invention around 1300, known as the flying buttress, helped medieval builders create soaring cathedrals like Notre Dame.

What is a flying buttress? A free-standing beam, the flying buttress bears the weight of a building's stone walls. The beam connects with a stone pier, spreading the structure's weight evenly.

In Gothic architecture, the flying buttress meant builders could design even taller structures. It also meant they could cut elaborate stained glass windows into the walls of cathedrals. Unlike earlier cathedrals, which were often dark inside, cathedrals with flying buttresses were airy and light.

1300: EUROPEANS CREATE PORTOLAN CHARTS, A NEW STYLE OF MAPMAKING.

In 1270, King Louis IX of France joined a French fleet on crusade. When a storm arose, scattering the ships, the king called for a map. His officers brought a portolan chart, a new style of mapmaking that emphasized coastlines.

Portolan charts drew the Mediterranean coast, sometimes extending to the Black Sea and the Atlantic. Along the coasts, mapmakers labeled every port. They left the land bare—these charts were meant for seafaring, not for crossing land.

Unlike earlier medieval maps, which offered more symbolic depictions of the world, the portolan charts prized realism. After all, sailors needed to know about marine hazards and the nearest ports. By the 15th century, the portolan style influenced how Europeans saw the world around them.

1305: GIOTTO PAINTS THE INTERIOR OF THE SCROVEGNI CHAPEL IN PADUA.

In 1305, a wealthy banker in Padua hired the artist Giotto to paint the interior of the family chapel. The Scrovegni family was known throughout Italy for fleecing borrowers with high interest rates, and the chapel would atone for the family's sins.

Today, the Scrovegni Chapel is famous for its frescoes. Giotto painted the entire interior of the chapel in rich blues and golds. The paintings show the lives of Jesus and the Virgin Mary, chronicling the wedding day of Joseph and Mary, Jesus's baptism, and the betrayal of Judas.

In a new and detailed style, Giotto infused his images with emotion, showing the anger on Jesus's face as he cast out the money lenders. Many point to Giotto's paintings as the birth of the Renaissance.

1306: ROBERT THE BRUCE, HIDDEN IN EXILE, LEARNS A VALUABLE LESSON FROM A SPIDER.

Crowned King of Scots in 1306, Robert the Bruce soon had to flee his homeland as the English invaded. Forced into hiding, his family captives of the English, Robert spent months alone in a desolate cave.

According to one story, the exiled king watched a spider for days. While weaving a web, the spider fell again and again. But every single time, it climbed the wall to keep trying. Finally, the spider succeeded.

Robert the Bruce identified with the spider—and used that as an inspiration to continue fighting the English. Although the odds were against the Scottish, Robert the Bruce succeeded in winning Scotland's independence.

1307: DANTE ALIGHIERI, FLORENTINE WRITER AND POET, BEGINS THE DIVINE COMEDY.

"Abandon all hope, ye who enter here." These words spanned the entrance to hell in Dante's Divine Comedy. In 1307, Dante himself felt hopeless. After devoting himself to Florentine politics for years, the city exiled him. While in exile, Dante wrote the *Divine Comedy*.

In his three-part epic poem, Dante traveled through hell, visited Purgatory, and ascended to paradise. Not shy about naming his enemies, Dante placed them in hell to suffer for eternity. He also coined dozens of new words and broke new theological ground in his poem.

Dante also married classical learning and Christianity. The Roman orator Cicero serves as Dante's guide on the journey, explaining that Christians can learn much from antiquity. Dante thus helped usher in the Italian Renaissance.

1314: KING ROBERT THE BRUCE WINS AGAINST THE ENGLISH AT BANNOCKBURN.

When King Edward II invaded Scotland, he brought over 25,000 men. Scotland's self-proclaimed king, Robert the Bruce, had only 6,000 men. But in the Battle of Bannockburn, the Scots won a victory that set them on the path to independence.

But the battle nearly went the other way. Early on the morning of the battle, an English knight named Sir Henry de Bohun caught sight of Robert the Bruce and charged with his lance. Bruce leaped on a horse to meet the knight. In the clash, the Scottish king dodged the lance and slammed his battle ax into the knight's head.

Their king's bravery encouraged the Scottish, who beat enormous odds to defeat the English and win Scotland's independence.

1324: MANSA MUSA, KING OF THE MALI EMPIRE, IS THE RICHEST MAN ALIVE.

A massive caravan crosses the Sahara Desert. A hundred camels stretch into the distance, each weighed down with 300 pounds of gold dust. Behind them came ten thousand servants carrying red and gold banners. At the head of the caravan sits the richest man in history: Mansa Musa.

Mansa Musa ruled over the Mali Empire, which supplied nearly half of the world's gold.

In 1324, Mansa Musa arrived in Cairo, ready to show off his wealth. He tossed gold nuggets to children on the street and bought everything he desired in the markets. For three months, Mansa Musa lavished his riches on Egypt's capital—but the king's spending came at a high price for the Egyptians. Mansa Musa poured so much gold into Cairo's economy that he crashed the economy, causing the price of gold to plummet for over a decade.

1325: MOROCCAN EXPLORER IBN BATTUTA LEAVES HIS HOME TO TRAVEL THE WORLD.

Born in Morocco a generation after Marco Polo, Ibn Battuta spent 24 years traveling the world.

At 21 years old, Battuta left Morocco for a pilgrimage to Mecca. Once he reached the holy city, Battuta continued his travels to Mali, India, and China. In all, Battuta covered 75,000 miles on his journey, visiting 40 countries on three continents.

When he returned home, Battuta wrote a book about his travels. He survived a sinking ship and escaped a ruler who wanted to kill him. Battuta also reported on the strange customs and foods he found in distant parts of the world. Like Marco Polo, Battuta carried tales of China's unimaginable wealth back to the Muslim world.

1340: VENICE BEGINS CONSTRUCTION ON THE DOGE'S PALACE.

Dating back to the 8th century, the Venetians elected a doge to govern their island territory. In the 14th century, the Venetians built a new palace to house their Doge and the republic's government.

By the 14th century, Venice dominated Mediterranean trade. The republic had also conquered distant territories to rule as part of its empire. Thanks to their close connections with Constantinople, the Venetians designed their palace in Byzantine style. Mosaics and patterns marked the outside of the palace, wrapped in pink marble from Verona.

Later renovations added a courtyard, covered walkways, and an arcade to the building, creating a uniquely Venetian structure.

1340: WILLIAM OF OCKHAM DEVELOPS THE APPROACH KNOWN AS OCKHAM'S RAZOR.

A theologian and lecturer at the University of Oxford, William of Ockham came up with a new rule: "plurality should not be assumed without necessity."

The phrase, now known as Ockham's Razor, cautions us that the least complicated explanation is the most likely. When an event has two possible explanations, choose the simpler one. For example, if you hear a stampede of animals, it's more likely horses than zebras.

William of Ockham devoted his life to philosophy and theology. He wrote commentaries on scholastic texts—but applying logic to religion did land Ockham in trouble. In 1328, the pope asked Ockham to solve a dispute on the role of poverty in faith. The philosopher concluded that the pope's view was heretical, earning Ockham a powerful enemy.

1345: THE AZTECS CREATE A NEW CAPITAL ON AN ISLAND IN A LAKE.

In the 14th century, the Aztecs had many powerful rivals but no home-land. Driven out of their previous territory by enemies, the Aztecs wandered, looking for the perfect site for a new city.

Around 1345, the Aztec priests declared that the gods wanted them to settle where they found an eagle clutching a snake while perched on a cactus.

The Aztecs spotted the sign on a swampy island in the middle of Lake Texcoco. Since no one else wanted the land, the Aztecs turned it into a city, using the marsh as a defense against their enemies. That city grew into Tenochtitlan—today Mexico City—and eventually housed 200,000 people.

1345: THE PONTE VECCHIO IS BUILT ACROSS THE ARNO RIVER IN FLORENCE.

The Romans founded Florence in the time of Julius Caesar and built a narrow bridge across the Arno River. In 1345, after floods swept away several bridges, the Florentines built a new bridge of stone.

Now known as the Ponte Vecchio, or old bridge, merchants began renting shops on the bridge. At first, they sold fish caught in the river, until Florentines started complaining about the smell. The republic then encouraged goldsmiths and jewelers to set up shop on the Ponte Vecchio.

In the 16th century, Florence's Medici duke added a new adornment to the Ponte Vecchio: a secret passage that ran above the shops, connecting the Medici palace to the city's town hall.

1347: THE BLACK DEATH ARRIVES IN EUROPE

A dozen ships from the Black Sea landed in Sicily in late 1347. But they carried more than trade goods—these ships brought the plague to Europe. Over the next few years, the Black Death killed half of Europe's population.

The devastating epidemic upended society and ushered in major changes. With a labor shortage, Europeans pushed for new technologies that saved manpower. Many farmers switched from growing grain to raising animals on their land.

Even more importantly, the plague slowly ended serfdom in Western Europe. Peasants and laborers could demand higher wages thanks to the labor shortage, which translated into better living conditions. Many peasants who survived the Black Death could afford butter, meat, and ale for the first time.

1349: ITALIAN WRITER GIOVANNI BOCCACCIO BEGINS HIS DECAMERON.

Boccaccio lived through the Black Death—and the plague inspired his famous *Decameron*. A collection of one hundred stories told by a group of Florentines fleeing the city during the plague, the *Decameron* wrestled with virtue in a post-plague world. Boccaccio's storytellers often cast off earlier restrictions to find humor and pleasure in their lives.

"You must read, you must persevere, you must sit up nights, you must inquire, and exert the utmost power of your mind," Boccaccio wrote. "If one way does not lead to the desired meaning, take another; if obstacles arise, then still another; until, if your strength holds out, you will find that clear which at first looked dark."

1350: THE AZTECS BUILD CANALS AND CAUSEWAYS IN TENOCHTITLAN.

The city of Tenochtitlan rose from the swamp as the Aztecs created canals and raised roads to transform their muddy island into a major city. Like Venice, the Aztecs used boats to navigate their city, along with bridges to the mainland that they could withdraw during an attack.

The Aztecs met in the city's public square and marketplaces. The city's major marketplace could cater to 40,000 customers on feast days, while the central plaza included a pyramid to worship the gods and a court to play games.

By transforming the swamp into a city, the Aztecs turned themselves into a major force in Mesoamerica.

1351: IN ENGLAND, A NEW GAME EMERGES CALLED TENNIS.

In the 19th century, Victorians played tennis on grass courts and held the first competition at Wimbledon. Tennis first appeared in England around 1351. In its earliest version, players passed a ball back and forth by striking it with their hands. The earliest tennis balls were made out of wood, and players would open the game by calling out "tenez," giving the sport its name.

Tennis rackets did not appear until the 16th century. By that time, King Henry VIII had installed tennis courts at one of his palaces and tennis had become a popular game among nobles across Europe. For centuries, tennis went by the name "royal tennis."

1364: PADUA BUILDS A LARGE CLOCK WITH MECHANICAL REGULATIONS.

In 14th-century Italy, the Paduans built a massive astronomical clock in their central piazza. The clock's dial would swing a full circle every 24 hours, striking out the hours starting with "zero hour."

The mechanical clock was both a technical and artistic marvel. The dial revealed the date, the moon's phase, and the position of the planets. Astrology lovers could look at the zodiac signs on the clock—with one exception. The clock left off the sign for Libra. Stories claim the builder intentionally excluded the sign as a slight on the city for shorting his bill. In fact, medieval astrologers often combined Scorpio and Libra.

1378: IN FLORENCE, THE CIOMPI REVOLT DEMANDS VOTING RIGHTS.

Florence gave voting rights to men who joined the city's guilds. But the lowest laborers were shut out of elections. In 1378, Florence's ciompi, or wool carders, revolted. They demanded voting rights in the republic and economic concessions from elected rulers.

After chanting in the streets and waving flags, the ciompi garnered several promises from the city's elected rulers. Not content with these promises from Florence's Signoria, the laborers installed one of their own members in a key government office.

The Ciompi Revolt was short-lived, however, as the major guilds soon returned to power. However, the Florentine laborer's revolt represents a unique expansion of a republic's voting body in the 14th century.

1381: THE PEASANTS' REVOLT IN ENGLAND DEMANDS RIGHTS FROM THE ARISTOCRACY.

The Italians weren't the only ones revolting in the wake of the Black Death. English peasants also rose up to demand better treatment from the nobility in 1381. The Peasants' Revolt started when a royal tax collector attempted to raise taxes on the country's farmers. In response, the peasants demanded concessions from England's aristocrats.

Led by Wat Tyler and John Ball, who declared that all Englishmen should be free and equal, the peasants marched to London. There, they met with King Richard II, just 14 years old. The boy king vowed to end serfdom in England, a massive concession to the peasants.

The Peasants' Revolt showed the changing balance of power between England's laborers and the nobility. Although the peasants didn't receive everything they demanded, the popular uprising showed the power of collective action.

1386: SALISBURY CATHEDRAL INSTALLS A CLOCK THAT IS STILL WORKING TODAY.

Before mechanical clocks, the length of an hour varied depending on the year. Sundials counted longer hours in summer than in winter. But new mechanical clocks ticked down the minutes evenly, changing how medieval people thought about time.

In 1386, England's Salisbury Cathedral installed a mechanical clock made from iron. For centuries, it marked the hours and rang 24 times a day. But after the clock's tower was demolished in the 18th century, the clock sat unused in the cathedral.

After undergoing restoration, the clock still works today—although its bell is silent—making it one of the oldest still-working clocks in the world.

1387: GEOFFREY CHAUCER BEGINS WRITING THE CANTERBURY TALES.

A group of pilgrims meet in London. On their journey to Canterbury, they tell each other stories. The Wife of Bath weaves a tale about a less-than-noble knight, while a miller relates the affairs of a student at

Oxford. The group listens to tales of Athenian rulers and roosters named Chanticleer.

When Geoffrey Chaucer began The Canterbury Tales, he planned to write 100 stories—but he died with just 24 complete. Even in its incomplete form, the stories offer a window into English life after the Black Death. By inventing characters from every social order, Chaucer showed off his skills writing courtly poems, religious tales, satires, beast fables, and more.

1397: THE MEDICI FOUND THEIR BANK IN FLORENCE.

The Medici became Italy's most powerful family in the Renaissance. Patrons of the arts and rulers of Florence, the family owed everything to their bank. In 1397, Giovanni de' Medici founded the Medici bank, and within a generation, the Medici ruled all of Florence.

The Medici became the bankers to the pope and opened branches across Europe. Through innovations like letters of credit, a medieval version of a credit card, the Medici soon amassed a huge amount of wealth. They poured that wealth into the arts, sponsoring artists like Botticelli and Michelangelo.

Cosimo de' Medici and his grandson Lorenzo the Magnificent dominated Florence in the 15th century, building allies—and enemies—thanks to their bank.

THE AGE OF DISCOVERY (1400-1500)

1403: THE YONGLE ENCYCLOPEDIA ATTEMPTS TO CATEGORIZE ALL KNOWLEDGE.

After decades of Mongol rule over China, the Ming dynasty put the Chinese back in control. The Yongle Emperor, the third emperor during the Ming dynasty, dedicated himself to promoting Chinese culture and knowledge. In 1403, he requested a new encyclopedia that would collect all of China's knowledge.

The Yongle Encyclopedia eventually ran to nearly 23,000 chapters collected in over 11,000 volumes. Written out by hand, the encyclopedia collected traditional knowledge and copied important texts on history, agricultural techniques, and science.

The massive encyclopedia remained the longest encyclopedia in the world for over six centuries—until Wikipedia surpassed it in 2007.

1405: CHRISTINE DE PISAN PUBLISHES CITY OF LADIES.

She was the first woman to make her living as a writer. Christine de Pisan became a widow in her 20s, left to support three children and her mother. Christine turned to writing to support her family.

Unlike other 15th century writers who leaned heavily on the "damsel in distress" theme, Christine wrote about women who were content not to be saved. In one poem, she claimed that being alone "pleases me the best."

Throughout her works, Christine argued for the rights of women. In her most famous book, *The City of Ladies*, Christine celebrated the most illustrious women of the past, lauding their great deeds.

1405: ADMIRAL ZHENG HE OF CHINA SETS OUT ON HIS FIRST VOYAGE.

On his seven voyages across the sea, Admiral Zheng He explored India, Arabia, and Africa. The Ming dynasty's Yongle Emperor commanded the voyages as a way to learn about foreign powers and encourage trade. With a crew of 28,000 and 300 ships, Zheng He presented gifts to rulers across the Indian Ocean, inviting them to send ambassadors to the imperial court.

When the king of Sri Lanka tried to steal from Zheng He's ships, the admiral abducted the king and brought him back to China, where the king agreed to pay tributes. In another adventure, Zheng He captured a famous pirate, earning supporters throughout the Malacca Straits.

By bringing back giraffes, gold, and wealth to China, Zheng He demonstrated the value of building close relationships with other powers.

1406: EUROPEANS RECOVER THE ANCIENT GEOGRAPHY OF PTOLEMY.

For centuries, Ptolemy's maps were lost. But in 1406, an Italian named Jacopo d'Angelo created a translation of the *Geography*. For Renaissance men obsessed with classical knowledge, Ptolemy's works introduced new styles of mapmaking and pushed Europeans to add to his works.

Editions of Ptolemy's works in the 15th century usually contained a dozen maps, including Ptolemy's map of the world. Europeans quickly identified errors in the *Geography*, like an underestimation of the world's size that convinced Columbus to sail west to find Asia. During the Age of Discovery, European explorers and mapmakers corrected Ptolemy's maps and expanded them, revealing how much of the world was still unknown.

1409: A CLASH BETWEEN POPES LEAVES EUROPE WITH THREE POPES AT ONE TIME.

From 1378 until 1409, two popes both claimed to lead the Catholic Church. Both had been elected by the same cardinals, and both refused to step down. The rival popes battled from Rome and Avignon, tearing the church apart.

In 1409, a group of cardinals held the Council of Pisa to solve the crisis. The council officially deposed both popes and elected a new one. But when the first two popes refused to step down, the Catholic Church found itself with three popes.

For a decade, the crisis continued, convincing many Catholics that the church should simply eliminate the office of the pope completely.

1418: FLORENCE LAUNCHES A COMPETITION TO BUILD EUROPE'S FIRST DOME SINCE ANTIQUITY.

In the 13th century, the Florentines began building a massive cathedral. And it would have the largest dome in history to prove that Florence's cathedral was "more useful and beautiful, more powerful and honorable" than any other church.

But long after they finished the building, Florence faced a big problem: no one knew how to build a dome that stretched nearly 150 feet across and began 180 feet in the air.

In 1418, Florence launched a competition to find an architect who could build the dome. One architect suggested that rather than scaffolding, the city could fill the entire cathedral with dirt. By mixing in coins, Florence's citizens would surely remove the dirt once the dome was built.

Architect Filippo Brunelleschi won the competition with his plan for a dome within a dome—and successfully completed the project in 1436.

1420: IN BEIJING, CHINA'S NEW CAPITAL, THE FORBIDDEN CITY IS BUILT.

The Ming dynasty built a new palace in China's new capital of Beijing. Called the Forbidden City, the palace remains the largest and best-preserved imperial palace in the world.

It took one million workers a full 14 years to build the Forbidden City. The Ming rulers brought in over 100,000 craftsmen to create the palace's elaborate works of art.

The massive palace included the emperor's living quarters, vast gardens, nearly 1,000 buildings, and over 8,700 rooms. From 1420 until 1912, the Forbidden City served as the home for 24 emperors.

Why did the Ming emperors call their palace the Forbidden City? Only members of the imperial family could enter the city without permission—commoners and government officials needed an invitation.

1429: JOAN OF ARC ENDS THE SIEGE OF ORLÉANS.

A surprising figure, Joan of Arc, rose to power in France and turned the tide of the Hundred Years' War in 1429. A teenager born into a peasant family, Joan convinced France's king that the saints spoke to her. The king accepted the girl's divine mission and granted her a military title and a small force to command.

Joan rode for the city of Orléans, which had been besieged by the English for over six months. She managed to sneak past the English to bring much-needed supplies to the city and later led the charge that forced the English to retreat from the city.

Though the English accused Joan of witchcraft and heresy, her heroism helped the French win the Hundred Years' War.

1438: IN SOUTH AMERICA, PACHACUTI FOUNDS THE INCA EMPIRE.

The ninth ruler of the Incas, Pachacuti transformed his territory into an empire. As a young man, Pachacuti defended the Inca city of Cuzco from an attack, helping him rise to power. As a ruler, Pachacuti conquered lands in the Cuzco Valley and vastly expanded the territory controlled by the Inca.

But Pachacuti was more than a conqueror. He also created the systems that kept his empire strong for a century. Conquered people would pay the empire in labor or goods, helping the Inca build a massive network of roads. He built the storage houses that stockpiled food in case of a famine. The emperor also chronicled his peoples' history to make sure history would never forget the Inca.

1439: PORTUGAL SENDS SETTLERS TO THE UNOCCUPIED AZORES ISLANDS.

Around 1427, a Portuguese sailor stumbled upon a group of uninhabited islands in the Atlantic Ocean: the Azores Islands. Seeing an opportunity, the Portuguese quickly moved to colonize the Azores. In 1439, the first colonists landed on the islands of Santa Maria and Sao Miguel to found new settlements.

The Portuguese initially planted the Azores with cash crops like sugarcane and oranges. Like Madieras and the Canary Islands, the Portuguese stopped in the Azores on their voyages down the coast of Africa.

As the island chain's population grew, the Azores became a target for Atlantic pirates. The Spanish seized the islands for a short time before Portugal took back control in the 17th century.

1450: IN THE ANDES MOUNTAINS, THE INCAS CONSTRUCT MACHU PICCHU.

Nearly 8,000 feet above sea level, the Incas built the city of Machu Picchu. Cliffs and forests surround the city, hiding it from view. It's no surprise that Machu Picchu became known as the Lost City of the Inca.

But why did the empire's founder, Pachacuti, found Machu Picchu? Some believe the city was once a fortress or perhaps a retreat for the emperor. Others say the city in the clouds served a religious purpose and may have been a sacred place for the Inca.

At its height, fewer than 1,000 people lived in Machu Picchu, and all traced their lineage back to the monarch. The Inca abandoned the city for unknown reasons just years before contact with Pizarro and the Spanish conquistadors.

1453: THE OTTOMAN TURKS SUCCESSFULLY CAPTURE CONSTANTINOPLE

The Byzantine city of Constantinople, founded by the Roman emperor Constantine in the 4th century, protected itself with multiple thick sea and land walls. But in 1453, an Ottoman army stormed the walls and ended the Byzantine Empire.

Why did the Ottomans succeed where so many others had failed? The Ottomans had technology on their side. For weeks, they blasted the walls with cannons, including the largest cannon ever built. But old fashioned subterfuge ultimately won the day. On May 29, 1453, someone left a gate in the walls open, allowing the Ottomans to flood into the city.

Constantinople shifted from Byzantine to Ottoman hands, earning the city a new name: Istanbul.

1455: JOHANNES GUTENBERG PRINTS THE FIRST EUROPEAN BOOK USING MOVABLE TYPE.

In a small print shop in Germany, Johannes Gutenberg printed Europe's first book that used moveable type. The Gutenberg Bible became one of the most famous books in the world—and ushered in a new era for Europe.

Gutenberg printed his bible on paper and vellum, and many added hand-painted illustrations to imitate a medieval manuscript. Gutenberg and his associates laid down the type for each individual page in the printed book. Today, fewer than 50 copies of the Gutenberg Bible survive out of around 185 first-edition copies.

After the introduction of printing, the number of books in Europe skyrocketed. Literacy rates also increased, and the bible remained a best-seller for decades.

1462: AFTER CONQUERING CONSTANTINOPLE, MEHMED II BEGINS TO BUILD TOPKAPI PALACE.

When Mehmed the Conqueror rode into Constantinople, he had plans for his new capital. The Ottoman Empire would need a palace that matched the empire's power. Mehmed began building the Topkapi Palace in 1462.

The palace, which overlooks the Bosphorus Strait, housed the imperial court until 1856. Thirty sultans ruled from the palace, which included an imperial gate, several libraries, the imperial treasury, and elaborate kitchens that invented new treats for the emperor. The harem, elaborately decorated with tiles, sheltered dozens of women, including the emperor's female relatives, from inquiring eyes.

At its height, the palace required a staff of 4,000 to serve the Ottoman emperor.

1469: LORENZO DE' MEDICI TAKES CONTROL OF FLORENCE AT JUST 20 YEARS OLD.

Lorenzo de' Medici was only 20 years old when his father died, leaving Florence without a de facto ruler. But could Lorenzo step in to take his father's place? Ruling Florence was no easy task. A republic in name, the Medici governed from behind the scenes, pulling strings and rigging elections to maintain their power.

Within a decade, Lorenzo had established himself as Florence's ruler, surviving an assassination attempt that killed his brother. Although he vowed to "use constitutional methods as much as possible," others saw Lorenzo as a tyrant.

By turning powerful families into allies and sharing his wealth as a patron of the arts, Lorenzo transformed himself into Lorenzo the Magnificent.

1469: FERDINAND OF ARAGON AND ISABELLA OF CASTILE MARRY, UNIFYING SPAIN.

Aragon and Castile battled over the Iberian peninsula for centuries until a wedding united the powers. In 1469, Ferdinand of Aragon married Isabella of Castile, uniting Spain under a single crown.

On their wedding day, Ferdinand and Isabella were still teenagers. But by the height of their reign, they governed over a vast empire.

Ferdinand and Isabella changed Spain and shaped history—they introduced the Spanish Inquisition to maintain religious loyalty, pushed the Moors out of Grenada, and expelled the country's Jews and Muslims to create a unified Christian territory.

They also funded a long-shot voyage of exploration that turned the New World into Spain's largest province, setting in motion a colonial empire that would dominate the world for centuries.

1480: IN HIS TWENTIES, LEONARDO DA VINCI INVENTS THE PARACHUTE.

Leonardo da Vinci was more than an artist—he was also an inventor. Da Vinci's obsession with flight started early when he invented the first parachute. His invention, a wooden frame draped in cloth to slow someone's fall, would allow someone to "throw himself down from any great height without suffering any injury."

The parachute was just the start. Da Vinci also invented a flying machine inspired by the flight of birds and bats. The pilot would pedal a crank to flap the structure's wings. The artist also created a helicopter centuries before man mastered flight.

Did Leonardo's inventions work? As far as we know, da Vinci never tested the parachute. But when a modern skydiver put the invention to the test, he declared it smoother than today's parachutes.

1480: BOTTICELLI PAINTS THE BIRTH OF VENUS AND PRIMAVERA FOR HIS MEDICI PATRONS.

In the late 15th century, Botticelli was Florence's most famous painter. He worked for the wealthy Medici family, painting enormous canvases on classical themes.

Around 1480, Botticelli painted The Birth of Venus and Primavera. His life-sized painting of the goddess Venus emerging from the sea on a shell became one of the most famous works of the Renaissance. Botticelli signaled a new movement in art that married classical mythology and the courtly love tradition.

Botticelli wasn't the only artist who enjoyed the patronage of the Medici. Florence's wealthiest family also commissioned works from Leonardo da Vinci and a teenage Michelangelo.

1485: IN ENGLAND, HENRY VII MARRIES ELIZABETH OF YORK, ENDING THE WAR OF THE ROSES.

The War of the Roses tore England apart, pitting noble families against each other. But a wedding in 1485 ended the war. That year, Henry VII married Elizabeth of York, bringing together the feuding families.

The sister of a king, many saw Elizabeth as the true heir to the throne. But after the bloody Battle of Bosworth, Henry Tudor seized power. By marrying Elizabeth, Henry united the white rose of York with the red rose of Lancaster, solidifying his throne.

The union also established the Tudor dynasty. Elizabeth would give birth to Henry VIII, whose three children, Edward, Mary, and Elizabeth, followed as monarchs.

1488: PORTUGUESE NAVIGATOR BARTOLOMEU DIAS SAILS AROUND THE CAPE OF GOOD HOPE.

When the Mongols swept through Asia, Europe lost its Silk Road connection to the east. Traders in the Middle East also maintained a monopoly, raising the price for spices and luxury goods in Europe. In response, generations of explorers sought new routes to China and the riches of the far east.

In 1488, a Portuguese explorer named Bartholomeu Dias became the first European to sail around Africa's southern tip. In the 15th century, many Europeans believed Africa connected with Asia, creating a land-locked sea. Instead, Dias found the Indian Ocean, clearing a new path to the east.

Portugal's success helped spur their rivals the Spanish to invest in a riskier westward route to Asia.

1492: MARTIN BEHAIM CREATES THE WORLD'S FIRST GLOBE.

In 1492, a German artist and geographer created a globe representing the known world. Martin Behaim's globe showed Europe, Asia, and Africa—the only continents Europeans knew at the time.

Based primarily on Ptolemy's classical knowledge, the globe added more recent information from Marco Polo and Portugal's voyages along the coast of Africa. Behaim also made the common mistake of underestimating the size of the Earth, convincing Europeans that sailing to Japan from the Canary Islands would take a matter of weeks.

Behaim named his globe the *Erdapfel*, or "earth apple." But that same year, Columbus's voyages made Behaim's geographical knowledge out of date.

1492: CHRISTOPHER COLUMBUS ARRIVES IN THE AMERICAS FROM SPAIN.

When Columbus landed in the Bahamas, he found "very green trees and many ponds and fruits of various kinds." Trees blossomed in October and sweet smells wafted on the gentle Caribbean breezes. But the navigator didn't find the gold and spices he promised to bring back to Ferdinand and Isabella of Spain. Instead, Columbus stumbled upon a new hemisphere.

Columbus made four voyages to the New World, where he seized slaves from the Tani people to prove the profitability of his expeditions. For the rest of his life, Columbus insisted he had sailed to the islands off the coast of China.

1497: VASCO DA GAMA SAILS TO INDIA, WHERE HIS GIFTS DO NOT IMPRESS THE RULER.

While the Spanish raced to find a western route to China, the Portuguese continued to send ships east. In 1497, Vasco da Gama successfully reached India.

When da Gama and his crew arrived in Calicut, the Portuguese sailor handed the ruler a gift of "twelve pieces of striped cloth, four scarlet hoods, six hats, four strings of coral, a case of six wash-hand basins, a case of sugar, two casks of oil, and two of honey."

In response, the court burst into laughter. The king's advisors said that even the poorest merchant from Mecca brought better gifts. Ashamed, da Gama claimed he was more like an ambassador than a trader. The rebuke drove home how poor Europe seemed compared to the rest of the world.

1497: FLORENCE, UNDER THE SWAY OF SAVONAROLA, HOLDS A BONFIRE OF THE VANITIES.

A charismatic preacher rose to power in Florence after Lorenzo the Magnificent died. Savonarola shamed the Florentines for their obsession with luxury and wealth. On February 7, 1497, the friar convinced the city to burn their luxuries—which became known as the Bonfire of the Vanities.

What did Florentines toss to the flames? Elaborate dresses, mirrors, musical instruments, and cosmetics went into the bonfire. Savonarola also convinced Botticelli to throw several works of art into the fires. Burning these objects, associated with vanity, represented a cleansing for the city. Such vanities distracted Florentines from their faith, Savonarola claimed.

But the next year, Florence turned on Savonarola and burned him as a heretic.

1498: TOOTHBRUSHES APPEAR IN CHINA

The Chinese invented toothbrushes long before anyone else. Their toothbrushes, made from thick hog bristles set in a bamboo or bone handle, replaced the older chew stick. After chewing up the end of a twig, people used the edges to clean their teeth. Chew sticks dated at least back to 3500 BCE in Mesopotamia.

In 1498, a Ming emperor patented the toothbrush. Chinese toothbrushes took dental hygiene to a new level. Toothbrush makers would scour the empire for the best hog bristles, preferring those from hogs that lived in colder, Siberian places where their bristles grew thick and firm.

Soon, Japanese visitors to China brought the invention back to Japan, and the invention spread to Europe by the 17th century.

1501: IN FLORENCE, MICHELANGELO BEGINS WORKING ON THE STATUE OF DAVID.

The slab of Carrara marble had sat in Florence for decades. Two other sculptors had tried working with the pure white block and rejected it. Until Michelangelo, at 26 years old, took up his chisel.

That block of marble became the most famous sculpture in the world: Michelangelo's David. Standing 17 feet tall, the sculpture took the artist two years to perfect. David, a valiant young hero, stands ready to battle Goliath.

Originally, the Florentines planned to place the statue on top of their Duomo. But it was so magnificent—and heavy—that the republic placed the statue outside the town hall. David faced south, gazing down the road to Rome, where the exiled Medici bided their time before returning to Florence.

1503: LEONARDO DA VINCI BEGINS PAINTING THE MONA LISA.

The portrait sat in Leonardo da Vinci's studio for years. When the artist died in 1519, the Mona Lisa still sat on its easel.

Who was Mona Lisa, the mysterious woman in one of the most famous paintings in the world? The wife of a silk merchant, Lisa Gherardini sat for the portrait in 1503. Over the years, da Vinci returned to the painting, adding new layers of oil.

When the artist died, King Francis I of France added the Mona Lisa to his royal collection. It hung on the wall in Napoleon's bedroom. In the early 19th century, the Mona Lisa moved to the Louvre Museum, where six million people visit it each year.

1508: IN ROME, MICHELANGELO PAINTS THE SISTINE CHAPEL CEILING.

By 1508, Michelangelo was the most famous sculptor in the world. That year, Pope Julius II asked the artist to paint the ceiling of the Sistine Chapel, which had been built only a few years earlier.

Why did the pope hire a sculptor to paint? One 16th century rumor claimed that Raphael suggested Michelangelo for the job to show his rival's limits. But Michelangelo proved his skill with the brush by creating a stunning collection of scenes from the Old Testament, including the creation of Adam.

For four years, Michelangelo and a team of painters worked on scaffolding to decorate the ceiling. Decades later, another pope invited the artist back to paint the Last Judgment, transforming the entire chapel with Renaissance art.

1513: MACHIAVELLI WRITES THE PRINCE, AN INFLUENTIAL WORK OF POLITICAL PHILOSOPHY.

In 1512, the exiled Medici returned to Florence, overthrowing the republic and jailing their political enemies. One of those enemies was Niccolo Machiavelli, a political advisor who the Medici tortured before exiling him from the city.

To win back their favor, Machiavelli wrote *The Prince*, a guide to seizing and keeping power in the chaotic world of Renaissance Italy. Machiavelli advised rulers to act nobly while hiding their brutal, ruthless natures: "Everyone sees what you appear to be, few really know what you are."

Machiavelli also praised rulers who surrounded themselves with wise advisors.

"The first method for estimating the intelligence of a ruler is to look at the men he has around him"—a not-so-subtle hint to ask for a position in Florence. But the Medici, still suspicious of Machiavelli's loyalties, did not bring him back to their court.

1517: MARTIN LUTHER POSTS HIS 95 THESES, BEGINNING THE PROTESTANT REFORMATION.

"Why does not the pope, whose wealth today is greater than the wealth of the richest Crassus, build the basilica of St. Peter with his own money rather than with the money of poor believers?" In one question, Martin Luther broke with the Catholic Church and started the Protestant Reformation.

A monk, Luther nailed his 95 Theses to the door of a German church. His criticisms ranged from matters of theology to the practice of selling indulgences to void sin. Although he originally wanted to reform the church from within, Luther soon found himself as the leader of a new religious movement that permanently split Europe into Catholic and Protestant faiths.

1518: THE DIPLOMAT LEO AFRICANUS ARRIVES IN ROME AS A SLAVE.

While sailing from Egypt to Morocco, Spanish pirates captured the Arabic traveler and diplomat Leo Africanus. Taken to Rome as a slave, the traveler soon impressed Pope Leo X with his knowledge of the world. Within a year, the pope freed the slave, who took the name Leo to honor the pontiff.

Before arriving in Rome, Leo Africanus had traveled throughout the Mediterranean world, from Grenada to Timbuktu and Constantinople. He also studied at the university in Fez, Morocco before becoming a diplomat.

In Europe, Leo taught Arabic and educated Rome's scholars about Islam. In 1526, he wrote a book about Africa and later returned to Tunis, where he spent the rest of his life.

1518: THE MYSTERIOUS DANCING PLAGUE OF 1518 BEGINS IN STRASBOURG.

In the summer of 1518, Frau Troffea walked into the streets of Strasbourg and started dancing. Without a word, the woman danced for days, soon joined by dozens more. The dancers claimed they couldn't stop, moving as if in a trance.

The dancing plague soon spread to more than 400 people. Many collapsed from exhaustion, and some even died. Baffled, Strasbourg's physicians suggested "burning off" the dancing fever with more dancing, so the city brought in musicians to play for the dancers.

For more than two months, the dancing plague afflicted Strasbourg—until the city piled the dancers into wooden carts and hauled them to a mountaintop shrine, where they finally stopped dancing.

1519: MAGELLAN SETS OFF ON A VOYAGE TO CIRCUMNAVIGATE THE EARTH.

Magellan set sail with five ships in 1519, convinced that he could find the route to Asia by sailing around South America. Three years later, only one ship returned, with just 18 men from the original crew of 270.

On Magellan's voyage to circumnavigate the world, the crew explored Brazil, found the Strait of Magellan, and became the first European voyage to cross the Pacific Ocean. During the 99-day ocean crossing, the crew eventually resorted to chewing leather to survive.

Magellan himself died in the Philippines when a poisoned arrow struck him during a battle. But his remaining crew members successfully reached the Spice Islands, sailed across the Indian Ocean, and made their way back to Spain.

1523: HERNÁN CORTÉS INTRODUCES THE CACAO BEAN TO SPAIN.

Hernán Cortés marched into Mexico and met with Emperor Montezuma in the Aztec capital of Tenochtitlan. When the two met, the emperor introduced Cortés to a luxurious Aztec drink: chocolatl. Made from cacao beans and chili pepper, the conquistador instantly loved the drink.

When Cortés sailed back to Spain, he loaded his ship with cacao beans. The Spanish modified the recipe, adding sugar and cinnamon, and began serving the cocoa drink hot.

For a century, the Spanish maintained a monopoly on hot chocolate, refusing to give up the secret to their European rivals. In the 17th century, an Italian had to visit the Aztecs in Central America to learn the secret. Hot chocolate soon spread to Italy, France, the Dutch, Germany, and England.

1529: THE TREATY OF ZARAGOZA DRAWS A LINE DOWN THE PACIFIC.

In 1494, the pope drew a line down the Atlantic and told the Spanish to explore to the west while the Portuguese explored to the east. But by 1529, European explorers had crossed the Pacific, raising a new question: where did the line fall on the other side of the world?

At stake was the Moluccas, also known as the Spice Islands. The Portuguese claimed the prize fell in their hemisphere, while the Spanish printed maps showing the islands on their side.

Once again, the pope had to mediate the dispute. In the Treaty of Zaragoza, the Portuguese were allowed to trade in the Moluccas—but they had to pay the Spanish a fee since the pope thought Spain's maps were better.

1532: PIZARRO CAPTURES INCAN EMPEROR ATAHUALPA

It was the largest ransom in history. When conquistador Francisco Pizarro arrived in the Incan Empire, he brought 200 men to face down thousands. But Pizarro's steel weapons gave his side a massive advantage. The Spanish were able to defeat 5,000 Inca soldiers and capture Emperor Atahualpa without a single Spanish casualty.

The Spanish then held Atahualpa captive, demanding an enormous ransom from the Inca. To save their emperor, the Inca would need to fill an entire room with gold and a second room with silver.

Shockingly, the Inca paid off Pizarro—but the conquistador executed Atahualpa anyway, declaring that the emperor was worthless to the Spanish.

1533: ANNE BOLEYN BECOMES QUEEN OF ENGLAND

"Your wife I cannot be," Anne Boleyn told King Henry VIII, "because you have a queen already. Your mistress I will not be." For seven years,

Henry pursued Anne, who was one of Catherine of Aragon's maids of honor.

Henry wrote to Rome asking for an annulment in his first marriage. When the pope refused, the king broke with the Catholic church and declared himself single. Anne and Henry married in a secret ceremony and later crowned Anne the queen of England.

But the union didn't have a happy ending. In 1536, Henry accused Anne of incest, adultery, and treason. England's queen was executed— and Henry married his third wife 11 days later.

1543: COPERNICUS PUBLISHES HIS BOOK CLAIMING THAT THE EARTH REVOLVES AROUND THE SUN.

In 1513, a scholar named Nicolaus Copernicus came up with a new model for the solar system. Instead of placing the Earth at the center of the universe, Copernicus claimed the earth revolved around the sun.

Copernicus wasn't the first to propose the idea. Ancient Greek astronomers had proposed the same theory centuries earlier. But Copernicus knew his theory would run into problems with the Catholic Church, which argued the Earth was at the center of the universe.

As a result, Copernicus waited for 30 years to publish his work. It was only on the man's deathbed in 1543 that he gave permission to publish the book he called *On the Revolutions of the Celestial Spheres*.

1543: ANATOMIST ANDREAS VESALIUS PUBLISHES AN INFLUENTIAL BOOK ON HUMAN ANATOMY.

For centuries, surgeons and physicians relied on the great classical doctor Galen for anatomical information. But in 1543, Andreas Vesalius published a book that overturned classical medical knowledge.

Vesalius, a professor at the University of Padua, used human dissections to understand anatomy. To Vesalius, proof from his own eyes was more valuable than ancient medical texts. Through anatomical dissection, Vesalius proved Galen wrong in several areas.

The anatomist realized the value of art—for the illustrations in *On the Structure of the Human Body*, Vesalius visited Venice where he ordered images from Titian's studio. Thanks to his detailed anatomical knowledge, Vesalius showed that Renaissance men could surpass classical wisdom.

1550: FRENCH SURGEON AMBROISE PARÉ BEGINS CREATING ARTIFICIAL LIMBS.

He was the royal surgeon for four French kings. Ambroise Paré started his career as an army surgeon, where he treated battlefield injuries. Thanks to that training, Paré began experimenting with artificial limbs.

The surgeon knew how amputations affected soldiers, which drove his inventions. Unlike earlier artificial limbs, Paré's inventions incorporated mechanical components. He created knees for soldiers with amputated limbs that could actually bend. Paré also designed an arm that used a pulley system to move.

Long before modern prosthetics, the French surgeon created robotic inventions to change people's lives. Ambroise Paré also crafted artificial eyes from gold and invented scientific instruments.

1558: ELIZABETH TUDOR BECOMES QUEEN ELIZABETH I

She was the daughter of a witch and spent time in jail before becoming queen. When Anne Boleyn gave birth to Elizabeth Tudor and Henry VIII declared the child illegitimate, few thought Elizabeth would ever rule. But when her half-sister died, Elizabeth Tudor became Queen Elizabeth I.

Just four years before Elizabeth became queen, Mary Tudor suspected her sister of rebellion. Elizabeth spent time in prison before clearing her name.

Queen Elizabeth ruled for 44 years without ever marrying—breaking the tradition of her father, who married six times. As queen, she strengthened the Anglican church and defeated an attack from the Spanish Armada. Elizabeth also became an important patron of the arts, encouraging young Englishmen like William Shakespeare.

1559: AN ITALIAN INVENTS ICE CREAM

The powerful Medici family impressed Europe with their power, their wealth, and their ice cream. During a feast at a Medici palace in 1559, an architect introduced a new dessert. Bernardo Buontalenti created a recipe that mixed cream, honey, egg yolk, and citrus. The Medici loved the dessert, calling it the "Florentine Cream."

Buontalenti did more than invent ice cream. He also designed a machine to crank out massive amounts of the delicious treat.

Ice cream soon spread to other countries. In France, Queen Catherine de' Medici encouraged a taste for ice cream, and the Italian gelato quickly became a favorite treat across Europe.

1566: CHINESE EMPEROR JIAJING PURSUES AN ELIXIR FOR EVERLASTING LIFE.

For centuries, China's emperors searched for an immortality potion. The elixir of everlasting life would protect an emperor from death—if he could discover the exact recipe. But when the Ming emperor Jiajing took an immortality potion in 1566, he accidentally poisoned himself.

Jiajing ruled for over four decades. During that time, he took many doses of an immortality elixir prepared by his alchemists. But the potion contained a deadly ingredient—mercury. Jiajing wasn't the first or last Chinese emperor to die from alchemical elixir poisoning. Other emperors took doses of arsenic, sulfur, and other deadly metals that contributed to their death.

1569: CARTOGRAPHER GERARDUS MERCATOR PUBLISHES AN INFLUENTIAL WORLD MAP.

The Mercator projection still covers the walls of school classrooms centuries after the cartographer lived—convincing generations of students that Greenland matches Africa in size.

In 1569, Gerardus Mercator came up with a new way to draw the world. His system created straight lines of latitude and longitude, making it easier for navigators to track their location at sea. Earlier maps used curved lines, making it difficult for sailors to chart their location.

Mercator's projection distorted lands close to the poles, making Greenland and Antarctica look much larger than their actual size. But the mathematical and navigational benefits of Mercator's map made it influential for centuries.

1571: AFTER 2,500 YEARS, GALLEYS ROW INTO BATTLE FOR THE LAST TIME AT LEPANTO.

Galleys dominated warfare at sea for more than two millennia. The ancient Greeks rowed to war in their galleys, and Rome defeated Carthage thanks to the galley. But in 1571, galleys fought their last war: the Battle of Lepanto.

That year, the Ottoman Turks threatened to march through Europe, conquering Christian powers. A group of European powers that called themselves the Holy League confronted an Ottoman navy in the eastern Mediterranean.

The two sides lined up in the sea, with thousands of men ready to row into the battle. When the galleys reached each other, armed men fought from the decks of their ships. Over 400 ships clashed at Lepanto, making it one of the largest naval battles since antiquity.

During the showdown, the European navy captured 117 galleys while only losing 12 of their own galleys. But it was the last battle for the galley—soon, galleons powered by sail replaced the rowed galleys in naval warfare.

1576: DANISH ASTRONOMER TYCHO BRAHE BUILDS AN OBSERVATORY.

A young student named Tycho Brahe gave up his study of the law in 1560 when he witnessed a solar eclipse predicted by astronomers. The marvel convinced Brahe to study astronomy.

In 1576, Brahe built an observatory on a Danish island and named it Uraniborg after the muse of astronomy. From his observatory, Brahe studied the stars and invented new astronomical instruments. Brahe also waded into the Copernican controversy, suggesting that the other planets revolved around the Sun, which revolved around the Earth.

A generation before Galileo turned the telescope on the stars, Brahe measured the position of the heavens with the naked eye. The astronomer marked the location of nearly 800 stars during his career.

1580: IN NORTH AMERICA, FIVE TRIBAL GROUPS CREATE THE IROQUOIS LEAGUE.

The tribes of the northeast should come together to advance "peace, civil authority, righteousness, and the great law," a Huron leader called the Peacemaker said in the late 16th century.

Five tribes—the Mohawk, the Oneida, the Onondaga, the Cayuga, and the Seneca—came together to form the Iroquois League. Also known as the Iroquois Confederacy or the Five Nations, the tribes stood together to protect their land from invasions. Each tribe sent representatives to a council that voted, making the league one of the oldest participatory democracies in the world.

The Iroquois model inspired Benjamin Franklin to propose a similar confederacy for the American colonies. Unlike Franklin's model, the Iroquois Confederacy still exists today.

1582: THE NEW GREGORIAN CALENDAR JUMPS FROM OCT. 4 TO OCT. 15.

Easter fell on the wrong date. By 1582, errors in the Julian calendar had moved Easter so far from the spring equinox that the pope intervened. That year, Pope Gregory XIII introduced a new calendar that would more accurately match the length of a solar year.

But introducing a new calendar wasn't easy. The pope told Catholics to skip 11 days to catch up—calendars jumped from Oct. 4 to Oct. 15, with nothing in between.

While Catholic countries quickly made the switch, it took centuries for other western powers to adopt the Gregorian calendar, and not without resistance. When England's Parliament switched in 1752, Englishmen rioted and demanded that the government "give us our 11 days." Ben Franklin, on the other hand, quipped, "It is pleasant for an old man to be able to go to bed on September 2, and not have to get up until September 14."

1590: AN ENGLISH SHIP FINDS NO TRACES OF THE SETTLERS AT ROANOKE ISLAND.

In 1587, over a hundred English settlers created a permanent settlement on Roanoke Island, off the coast of North Carolina. The colony's governor left his family behind at Roanoke to return to England for supplies. But when his ship returned in 1590 to restock the settlement, the colony was deserted. There was no trace of the dozens of families— or young Virginia Dare, the first English settler born in North America—at Roanoke.

What happened to the Roanoke settlement? The only trace left behind was the word "Croatoan" carved into a post. Did the colonists abandon the settlement? Were they attacked? Did they try to return to England, only to be lost at sea?

Centuries later, the "lost colony" of Roanoke continues to puzzle people today.

1598: THE EDICT OF NANTES ENDS THE FRENCH WARS OF RELIGION.

For decades, the French fought viciously over religion. On the bloody St. Bartholomew's Day Massacre, France's Catholics slaughtered 3,000 Protestants in a single day.

But in 1598, King Henry IV ended the French Wars of Religion with the Edict of Nantes. The edict proclaimed religious tolerance throughout France. The Protestant minority, known as the Huguenots, could worship freely, attend universities, and own property in France.

Many suspected Henry IV of secretly holding Protestant beliefs. When he succeeded to the throne in 1589, beginning the Bourbon dynasty, Henry reportedly quipped "Paris is worth a mass" and converted to Catholicism. With the Edict of Nantes, France became one of the first European countries to promote religious tolerance.

1599: WILLIAM SHAKESPEARE BEGINS WRITING HAMLET

"To be, or not to be—that is the question." William Shakespeare's line in *Hamlet* remains one of the most famous phrases centuries later.

In 1599, the playwright William Shakespeare began building the Globe Theater and writing his most famous play—*Hamlet*. In the revenge tragedy, Shakespeare's hero chases his father's murderer, who just happens to be his uncle. The melancholy prince battles madness to unravel a crime committed in his own family.

Shakespeare wrote *Hamlet* in the middle of his career. He'd already written *Romeo and Juliet*, most of his historical plays, and *Twelfth Night*. In the final decade of his career, the playwright would pen *Othello*, *Macbeth*, and *King Lear*. Yet over 400 years later, *Hamlet* remains Shakespeare's most performed play.

THE SCIENTIFIC REVOLUTION (1600S)

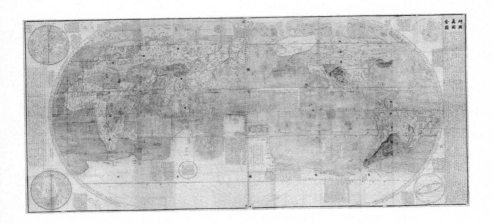

1602: MATTEO RICCI CREATES A WORLD MAP IN CHINA.

The Jesuit priest Matteo Ricci traveled to China in 1583, rising to become head of the Jesuit mission in China. While at the imperial court, Ricci collaborated with Chinese scholars to create an influential world map.

Ricci introduced European map-making techniques and geographical knowledge from a century of exploration. The Chinese scholars reshaped the world map to fit a Chinese outlook on the world. Unlike European world maps, the Ricci Map placed China in the center of the map. The map also praised China's emperor and lauded the country's power.

The map, which stretched 12 feet by 5 feet, represents an important collaboration between East and West.

1603: TOKUGAWA IEYASU TAKES THE TITLE SHOGUN, BEGINNING THE TOKUGAWA SHOGUNATE.

In the 16th century, warring factions tore Japan apart. Feudal lords battled for power—until one rose to create a new dynasty.

After winning the Battle of Sekigahara, Tokugawa Ieyasu transformed Edo (known as Tokyo today) into Japan's new imperial capital. He also began the Tokugawa shogunate, which would rule for over 250 years.

Japan's new rulers prioritized building cities and encouraging trade. Ieyasu placed limits on the power of feudal lords, ushering in a period of peace and stability. Early on, Ieyasu welcomed trade relationships with the Portuguese and Dutch. But the shogun soon began to rethink his relationship with Western powers, fearing that attempts to spread Christianity could disrupt the peace. Ieyasu eventually closed the country to European powers.

1605: GUY FAWKES ATTEMPTS TO BLOW UP PARLIAMENT IN THE GUNPOWDER PLOT.

"Remember, remember, the 5th of November." What, exactly, happened on Nov. 5, 1605? Or, rather, what *didn't* happen. That day, a conspiracy led by Guy Fawkes tried to blow up the Parliament building in London.

The Gunpowder Plot started when a group of Catholics decided to end Protestant rule—permanently. The conspirators filled the space below Parliament with 36 tightly-packed barrels of gunpowder. In the early hours of Nov. 5th, King James's chief minister stumbled upon Guy Fawkes, sitting beneath the House of Lords and holding a box of matches.

Although the conspiracy failed, Londoners celebrated by burning Guy Fawkes in effigy every year on Nov. 5th.

1606: THE DUTCH SPOT NORTHERN AUSTRALIA AND ASSUME IT IS A MASSIVE SOUTHERN CONTINENT.

The earth was a sphere—but an unbalanced sphere would surely fall over. For centuries, Europe's mapmakers balanced the land in the northern hemisphere by inventing continents in the southern hemisphere. Ptolemy added imaginary southern continents to his work, and so did nearly every other mapmaker for over a thousand years.

So when a Dutch ship spotted a massive landmass in 1606, they assumed it was the mythical southern continent. Later European voyagers simply named the new continent Australia, after the Latin word "australis" which meant southern. The discovery made it easy for Europeans to update their maps, since they had already marked *Terra Australis* on centuries of maps.

1609: JOHANNES KEPLER DISCOVERS THE ELLIPTICAL ORBIT OF THE PLANETS.

The planets circulated in perfect spheres, revealing the order of the universe—until Johannes Kepler. In 1609, Kepler realized that the planets did not orbit on circular paths. Instead, they traveled in elliptical orbits.

Who was Johannes Kepler? The German astronomer worked with colleagues like Tycho Brahe and Galileo Galilei to overturn centuries of received wisdom about the universe. The theory of the perfection of the heavens dated back to Plato and the ancient Greeks.

Kepler created new laws of planetary motion, describing how the solar system operated. These laws put him firmly in the Copernican camp: Kelper argued that the planets orbited around the Sun, not the Earth.

1609: THE FIRST NEWSPAPERS APPEAR IN GERMANY

As far back as the Romans, newsletters spread important information throughout the empire. But it wasn't until the 17th century that newsletters evolved into the first newspapers.

Scholars trace the shift back to Augsburg, where a trading family called the Fuggers began circulating regular newsletters with financial information, political news, and any other topic that might influence the economy.

In Strasbourg, a publisher began printing a regular newspaper in 1609, and the idea quickly took off. The Dutch, master printers and traders, soon began publishing newspapers on international news.

These early newspapers typically came out once or twice a week. Thanks to the invention of printing, it was cheaper and easier than ever to report the news.

1610: GALILEO GALILEI OBSERVES THE SKIES WITH A TELESCOPE.

The telescope transformed Galileo Galilei's life. When he heard reports of a Dutch eyeglass maker who created a telescope, Galileo sat down to make his own homemade telescope. And on the night of January 7, 1610, Galileo turned his invention on the skies.

Galileo's telescope revealed secrets in the stars that no one had seen before. The moon's surface was not smooth, as ancient astronomers claimed, but covered in peaks and valleys. The sun's surface was covered in sunspots. And hidden celestial bodies appeared for the first time in Galileo's telescope, including the moons of Jupiter.

The discoveries confirmed Copernicus's theory—and set Galileo on a path toward his clash with the Catholic Church.

1614: THE FIRST BARRELS OF CURED TOBACCO REACH ENGLAND FROM VIRGINIA.

Sir Francis Drake brought two New World plants back to England after his 16th-century voyages: the potato and tobacco. The English initially tossed out the potato, believing it was poisonous. But tobacco soon became one of the most important New World crops.

By 1614, English settlers in Virginia were sending tobacco back to England by the barrel. Within ten years, Virginians were shipping 200,000 pounds of tobacco to England—and by 1680 Jamestown produced more than 25 million pounds of tobacco to sell in Europe.

Europeans declared tobacco a medicinal cure, with one Englishman even arguing that physicians were trying to keep tobacco a secret because it would destroy their business.

1619: ENGLISH SETTLERS IN VIRGINIA BUY ENSLAVED AFRICANS.

The first enslaved Africans in the English colonies arrived in 1619. A year earlier, a Portuguese ship kidnapped hundreds of men and women from villages in Angola. Half died during the Middle Passage. Another 50 were captured by English pirates on a ship called the White Lion.

The White Lion docked in Jamestown with 20 kidnapped slaves for sale. John Rolfe recorded the transaction, reporting "20 and odd Negroes" which the captain traded for food and supplies.

What happened to the first Africans brought to the American colonies as slaves? The records say little about their lives—but for the next 250 years, slavery would become a stain on America.

1620: FRANCIS BACON INTRODUCES THE SCIENTIFIC METHOD IN NOVUM ORGANUM.

Aristotelian science was broken, Francis Bacon declared. Undermined by evidence from telescopes and microscopes, Aristotle's method no longer provided reliable knowledge. As a result, Bacon announced, scientists would need to "make a general renewal of the sciences and arts and of all human learning."

But how? Bacon proposed a method for testing hypotheses using experiments. Scientists would manipulate nature and gather evidence, repeating their experiments again and again. Drawing on his legal background, Bacon likened investigating nature to a trial. Could scientists prove their hypothesis beyond a reasonable doubt?

Bacon's proposal became known as the scientific method and played a central role in the Scientific Revolution.

1624: THE JAPANESE IMPOSE NEAR TOTAL ISOLATION, BANNING TRAVEL AND VISITORS.

In 1624, Japan's era of Sakoku, or "closed country," began. That year, Japan banned Europeans from the country to prevent foreign intervention or colonialism.

Although the Japanese allowed one Dutch outpost in Nagasaki, otherwise Japan closed itself to Western nations. Western powers could not trade with Japan. Diplomats and Christian missionaries were not welcome in the country. And most common Japanese people were banned from leaving the country. Japan remained closed until 1853.

The Sakoku era would strengthen traditional Japanese customs, rulers proclaimed. The Sakoku era saw the development of haiku poetry, the Japanese tea ceremony, bonsai cultivation, and wood-block prints. Japan also invested in its relationships with Korea and China.

1628: WILLIAM HARVEY PUBLISHES HIS THEORY ON THE CIRCULATION OF BLOOD.

The liver produced blood, which the heart burned up like a furnace. At least, that's what Galen and the classical medical authorities claimed. In 1628, an English doctor named William Harvey came up with a new theory based on his anatomical dissections. The blood circulated through the body.

Harvey's breakthrough theory started with a mathematical proof. If the heart burned up blood with each heartbeat, Harvey calculated, the body would need to make around 500 pounds of blood each day—clearly impossible.

In his book, Harvey laid out a new theory. The heart pumped blood through the body's arteries, and blood returned to the heart through the veins. Thanks to years of dissections and animal vivisections, Harvey unlocked important medical knowledge.

1633: TULIPMANIA TAKES OVER HOLLAND

The price of tulip bulbs skyrocketed in the early 17th century. Soon, traders were bidding thousands of florins—up to six times the average annual salary—on bulbs.

Why did tulip mania take over Holland? In the early speculative market, rare tulip bulbs became a hot commodity, creating a market bubble. Tulips from the Ottoman Empire were new to Europe, and the fashion for colorful hybrid tulips drove demand.

In Amsterdam's stock exchange, buyers bid up the price of bulbs until eventually the bubble burst. Buyers who had purchased bulbs on credit had to liquidate their holdings to avoid bankruptcy.

Tulip mania was the first market bubble—and it was followed by the South Seas bubble in the 18th century, the 1929 Wall Street crash, and the Dot com bubble.

1633: THE INQUISITION PUTS GALILEO ON TRIAL

In 1616, a Catholic cardinal warned Galileo not to teach that the Earth rotated around the sun. Why did the Catholic Church care so much about astronomy? Theologians pointed to the Bible, which claimed the sun stood still during a battle, as proof of the Earth's position at the center of the universe. By challenging that theory, Galileo rebelled against the church, according to the scientist's detractors.

In the context of the Protestant Reformation, the Catholic Church saw Galileo as a threat to their authority. The Inquisition eventually found Galileo guilty of heresy for arguing against scripture. The scientist was sent to house arrest, where he lived out the final years of his life.

In 1992, the Vatican formally apologized to Galileo and cleared his name.

1637: VENICE OPENS THE FIRST OPERA HOUSE, THE TEATRO DI SAN CASSIANO.

Italians invented opera—and Venice opened the first opera house in 1637. The Teatro di San Cassiano welcomed all to hear operas, encouraging the new performing art.

One of Venice's wealthiest families funded the opera house, intentionally opening the doors to all rather than restricting access to the nobility. Baroque operas pioneered lush, ornate sets and soaring arias. Venetians also clamored to hear castrati, or castrated male sopranos, and *prima donnas*. Venetian operas told the story of the city's noble past, sung of heroes from Greece and Rome, and entertained audiences with elaborate comedies.

By 1700, Venice had eleven opera houses, transforming the floating city in the opera capital of the world.

1637: PIERRE DE FERMAT FORMULATES FERMAT'S THEOREM

The French mathematician Pierre de Fermat devoted his life to studying numbers—but he refused to publish his findings. Fermat wrote to many leading mathematicians, including Blaise Pascal, but he felt publishing took time away from his work. Thanks to his correspondence with Pascal, scholars today credit Fermat for co-founding the field of probability.

But Fermat remains most famous for Fermat's Theorem, an equation he scrawled into the margin of a book. Fermat claimed that the equation $x^n + y^n = z^n$ had no solution if n is greater than 2. "I have discovered a truly remarkable proof which this margin is too small to contain," Fermat scrolled.

After Fermat's son published the note in 1670, mathematicians spent decades searching for a solution. In 1995, the British mathematician Andrew Wiles finally proved Fermat's Theorem.

1638: BAROQUE PAINTER ARTEMISIA GENTILESCHI PAINTS A SELF-PORTRAIT.

She was the most famous female painter of the 17th century. The daughter of an artist, Artemisia Gentileschi overcame tragedy to build her name as a painter.

Gentileschi's works included powerful scenes of Biblical women, including Judith slaying Holofernes, Jael, Mary Magdalene, and Bathsheba. She also painted historical women like Cleopatra and Lucretia.

Artemisia won acclaim from the Medici and other artists. She became the first woman in Florence's Academy of the Arts of Drawing. In 1638, Artemisia painted a self-portrait of herself as the Allegory of Painting. By depicting herself as the embodiment of painting itself, Artemisia argued that women could succeed in many male-dominated fields.

1643: AT JUST FOUR YEARS OLD, LOUIS XIV BECOMES KING OF FRANCE.

His royal parents named their son Louis-Dieudonné, or Louis, the gift of God. Before young Louis's fifth birthday, his father died, making the child the King of France. Louis would rule for the next 72 years as the Sun King.

A decade after becoming king, Louis took control of his throne, taking the place of his mother, Queen Anne of Austria, and his regent, Cardinal Mazarin.

Louis XIV saw himself as a ruler with absolute power. He transformed a disorganized kingdom of 20 million into a centralized power. By tying the nobility to the crown, Louis limited threats to his power. And although he spent money wildly, the Sun King also improved his country's finances.

The Sun King ruled for so long that he outlived his heirs. When he died in 1715, Louis's grandson became the new king.

1649: ENGLAND EXECUTES KING CHARLES I FOR TREASON.

It was the first—and only—time England executed a king. As monarch, King Charles I tried to rule with absolute power, but he earned many enemies, including in Parliament. Claiming a Divine Right to rule, Charles refused to listen to Parliament on taxation. He even dissolved Parliament multiple times to rule alone, refusing to let Parliament meet for 11 years.

Charles's clash with Parliament triggered a civil war. After years of war, the Royalists lost. In 1646, Oliver Cromwell placed the king under arrest and put him on trial for treason and tyranny. Charles claimed that his divine right placed him above the law, refusing to recognize the court.

The court found Charles guilty, and three days later Londoners gathered to watch the royal execution. A decade later, Charles's son would storm back into power and hunt down the men who executed his father.

1650: MASSACHUSETTS POET ANNE BRADSTREET PUBLISHES HER WORKS.

She became the first published poet from the American colonies. Anne Bradstreet found time to write poems while raising eight children and running a household in the Massachusetts colony. Born in England, Bradstreet moved to Massachusetts in the 1630s, where she found few of the comforts of the Old World.

A Puritan, Bradstreet mused about faith, sin, and salvation in her poems. The poet also captured her love for her family and community, writing about what it meant to be a woman.

In one poem, dedicated to Queen Elizabeth, Bradstreet also praised womankind. "Let such as say our Sex is void of Reason," Bradstreet penned, "Know tis a Slander now, but once was Treason."

1651: THOMAS HOBBES PUBLISHES HIS THEORY OF HUMAN NATURE AND POLITICAL POWER.

In a state of nature, man's life is "nasty, brutish, and short," declared English philosopher Thomas Hobbes. In his book *Leviathan*, Hobbes revealed an intensely negative view of human nature. Men were greedy and selfish, and only a ruler with absolute power could bring order to society.

Laws and power kept unruly men in line—and provided the only defense against murder and theft, according to Hobbes. An absolute ruler would impose harsh penalties on men, scaring them into submission.

Hobbes's dark political theories mirrored the bloody experience of the English Civil War, which convinced the philosopher of the necessity of an all-powerful ruler.

1652: IN LONDON, THE FIRST COFFEE HOUSE OPENS.

Pasqua Roseé, a Greek immigrant, opened London's first coffee house in 1652. At first, Londoners rejected the bitter drink from the Ottoman Empire. One critic dismissed coffee as "bitter Mohammedan gruel", while the Women's Petition Against Coffee called the drink a "newfangled, abominable, heathenish liquor called coffee."

But soon Londoners flocked to Pasqua's coffee house, where he served up 600 cups a day. The coffee house became a meeting place in London, and by 1663 nearly one hundred coffee houses sprung up in the city. King Charles II tried to shut down coffee houses, concerned about potentially treasonous talk, but the effort failed. Coffee houses became a permanent fixture in London.

1660: SAMUEL PEPYS BEGINS HIS DIARY

On January 1, 1660, Samuel Pepys opened up a diary and scrawled out his first entry. For the next decade, Pepys would record his thoughts on politics, the visitors to his household, and his finances. He also recorded several affairs with actresses he met in local theaters.

Pepys's diary chronicled England's plague of 1665 and the Great Fire that destroyed London in 1666. In over a million words, Pepys captured life in England, making his diary a critical source for historians. The diary also provides a window into daily life, as Pepys recorded what he ate each day and complained about the cat who woke him in the night.

1662: CHARLES II GRANTS A ROYAL CHARTER TO THE ROYAL SOCIETY.

"Take nobody's word for it." That was the motto of the Royal Society, London's leading scientific society.

In 1660, the scientist Christopher Wren gave a lecture at Gresham College. Afterward, he met with other natural philosophers who wanted to create a "College for the promoting of Physico-Mathematical Experimental Learning." In 1662, King Charles II granted the group a royal charter.

The Royal Society dedicated itself to the experimental method proposed by Francis Bacon. Its members, including Robert Hooke, Robert Boyle, and Isaac Newton, made groundbreaking discoveries about nature, from the microscope to the laws of motion. The Royal

Society also began publishing peer-reviewed papers in the first scientific journal in the world.

1663: ROBERT HOOKE DISCOVERS CELLS WITH A MICROSCOPE.

Galileo turned the telescope on the heavens in the early 17th century—and by the mid-17th century, scientists were using microscopes to learn about the invisible world.

In 1663, English scientist Robert Hooke used a microscope to observe a piece of cork. Although the piece looked solid to the naked eye, Hooke saw tiny compartments he named cells. To Hooke, these microscopic pockets looked like the cells in a monastery, inspiring the name.

"I could exceedingly plainly perceive it to be all perforated and porous, much like a honeycomb, but that the pores of it were not regular," Hooke recorded. "These pores, or cells, were indeed the first microscopical pores I ever saw, and perhaps, that were ever seen, for I had not met with any Writer or Person, that had made any mention of them before this."

1664: LOUIS XIV BEGINS BUILDING THE PALACE AND GARDEN AT VERSAILLES.

A magnificent king needed a magnificent palace. In 1664, the Sun King began building a palace to match his prestige—Versailles.

Once a royal hunting lodge, Louis XIV transformed Versailles into a majestic palace. With a hall of mirrors, wings for the king and queen, and a royal chapel, all gilded in gold, Versailles stunned visitors. The lavish gardens, outfitted with elaborate fountains and dotted with ancient statues and grottos, provided a pastoral setting for the palace.

In 1682, the king ordered the entire French court to move in, bringing aristocrats under his control. Versailles, which cost the Sun King millions of *livres*, became the most visible emblem of the king's absolute power and authority.

1665: ISAAC NEWTON DEVELOPS A THEORY OF GRAVITY.

In 1665, the plague swept across England. In response, Cambridge University sent students home, including a young Isaac Newton. For the next year, Newton conducted experiments in his small country village.

Newton's experiments began with optics and light. Soon he moved on to mathematics and calculus. Finally, he examined the natural laws that governed the universe, developing a mathematical theory of gravity. Though it would take Newton decades to publish his findings, the scientific leaps

"In those days I was in the prime of my age for invention," Newton later recalled of his *annus mirabilis*, or "year of wonders."

1666: THE GREAT FIRE OF LONDON BURNS THE CITY TO THE GROUND.

The Great Fire of London left more than 80% of the city in ruins. But after the fire, Londoners built back stronger than ever.

The fire started on September 2, 1666. When the city's mayor first heard of the fire, he dismissed it, scoffing, "A woman might piss it out!" But the blaze soon spread, finding fuel from London's many wooden structures. Within days, the fire destroyed 13,000 homes and St. Paul's Cathedral.

In the wake of the disaster, Londoners committed to rebuilding the city. The architect Christopher Wren drew up a new, more modern plan for the city's streets and buildings. He also designed the new St. Paul's Cathedral. Although the fire had left thousands homeless, London quickly recovered.

1667: THE FIRST HUMAN BLOOD TRANSFUSIONS TAKE PLACE IN FRANCE AND ENGLAND.

Long before doctors understood blood types, scientists conducted the first human blood transfusions in the 17th century. But they didn't use human donors for the blood—instead, they transfused animal blood into human subjects.

In Paris, a physician transfused sheep's blood into several patients—

134

and two died. The physician ended up on trial for murder. In England, the Royal Society transfused lamb blood into Arthur Coga, who claimed the procedure transformed him into a sheep-man.

Why did 17th-century scientists use animal blood? They saw using human blood as unethical, because the donor often died from blood loss. After multiple unsuccessful experiments, England and France both banned blood transfusions.

1670: JAPANESE POET MATSUO BASHO WRITES THE FIRST HAIKUS.

Born in Kyoto, Matsuo Basho became one of Japan's most celebrated poets. After studying Chinese poetry, Basho developed a new style that would define Japanese poetry for centuries: the haiku.

> *On a withered branch*
> *A crow has alighted:*
> *Nightfall in autumn.*

Basho's poetry was more than a repeated pattern of syllables. He focused on nature, writing about frogs leaping into ponds, the first snow-fall of winter, and falling cherry blossoms. The poet drew from his own experiences, writing about a 1,200-mile walk across Japan. By focusing on the natural world and its slow transformations, Basho highlighted the contemplative power of verse.

1676: ANTONIE VAN LEEUWENHOEK DISCOVERS BACTERIA

The microscope unlocked a new world to explore. In 1676, the Dutch shopkeeper Antonie van Leeuwenhoek started grinding lenses in his free time to investigate the microscopic world. He became the first to observe bacteria, which he called animalcules, or tiny animals.

After discovering multi-celled bacteria, Leeuwenhoek also identified single-celled bacteria, red blood cells, and protozoa. How did Leeuwenhoek, who ran a drapery, become the Father of Microbiology? His self-taught skill as a microscope maker gave the draper the power to magnify nature by 300 times.

Like other experimentalists in his time, Leeuwenhoek did not publish his findings. Instead, he wrote letters to the Royal Society in London, which circulated the remarkable discovery.

1682: EDMOND HALLEY CHARTS THE PATH OF HALLEY'S COMET.

While 17th-century microscopes revealed a teeming world of life, telescopes uncovered a shocking number of stars—and comets—in the sky.

Before Edmond Halley, many assumed comets were signs from God—and they usually brought bad luck. In 1664, a comet appeared above the city of London. The next years brought plague and fire.

But Halley proved that comets followed the same celestial laws as planets. Comets, like planets, traveled on orbits. The astronomer argued that the comets that appeared in 1531, 1607, and 1682 were actually the same comet returning—and it would come back in 1758.

Halley's prediction came true after his death, and today the comet carries his name: Halley's comet.

1687: ISAAC NEWTON PUBLISHES HIS PRINCIPIA MATHEMATICA

In 1684, astronomer Edmond Halley visited Isaac Newton with a problem: could you mathematically describe the orbital paths of planets? Newton responded that he'd solved the problem years ago, sharing his equations with Halley. Stunned, Halley encouraged Newton to publish his theories.

When Isaac Newton determined the law of gravity and the three laws of motion, he kept them to himself. At first unwilling to face criticism or defend his theories, Newton simply continued studying nature rather than sharing his findings with the scientific community.

But in 1687, Newton published his masterful *Principia Mathematica*, which introduced the Newtonian laws of motion and his law of universal gravitation. Though the book contained complicated mathematical ideas, its groundbreaking findings shaped science for centuries.

1689: ENGLAND PASSES A BILL OF RIGHTS

After a civil war and the overthrow of two monarchs, England longed for political stability. In 1689, the English Bill of Rights transformed the country into a constitutional monarchy with Parliament firmly in control.

William and Mary signed on to the Bill of Rights after ousting King James II. Although the Bill of Rights limited the power of monarchs, it helped secure their rule. The Bill of Rights spelled out the powers of Parliament and declared freedom of speech, the right to bear arms, freedom from cruel and unusual punishment, and the right to a trial.

The English Bill of Rights inspired the U.S. Bill of Rights a century later.

1698: PETER THE GREAT DISGUISES HIMSELF AS A COMMONER TO LEARN ABOUT WESTERN EUROPE.

Russia's king wanted to learn more about the West. So Peter the Great disguised himself to travel through Europe incognito.

On the Grand Embassy, Peter the Great visited Amsterdam where he worked in a shipyard learning how the Dutch built ships that circled the globe. In Britain, the king toured factories and dockyards to learn about English technologies.

The disguise didn't fool many—the king was a towering 6 feet 8 inches tall. Still, the king returned home after the Grand Embassy convinced that Russia needed to modernize if it wanted to compete with Europe. He even passed a law against growing beards to imitate the Western style.

THE AGE OF REVOLUTION (1700S)

1709: BARTOLOMEO CRISTOFORI BUILDS THE FIRST PIANO.

The Medici family hired a man from Padua to care for their harpsichords in 1688. That man, Bartolomeo Cristofori, later built the first piano.

The piano's inventor spent years studying instruments as he cared for them, tinkering with adjustments to the strings, the hammers, and the other tools within the instruments. Thanks to his hands-on study, Cristofori created pianos that other instrument makers couldn't improve on for the next 75 years.

Cristofori's piano delighted audiences, who marveled at its ability to play soft and loud—or "piano e forte" in Italian. The playing style gave the invention the name pianoforte, and later piano.

1712: THOMAS NEWCOMEN INVENTS THE STEAM ENGINE

England's mines kept filling with water. In response, Thomas Newcomen invented a steam engine to keep the mines running.

Newcomen's invention pumped water from the bottom of the mines up to the surface using an engine powered by steam. The innovation kept the coal and iron mines running. Soon the English came up with new uses for the engine. They could drain water from the wetlands or pump water into towns. The steam engine could also pump water to power factories.

By unlocking the power of the mechanical engine, Newcomen ushered in the Industrial Revolution. Soon, his steam engine powered manufacturing across Europe.

1717: LADY MARY WORTLEY MONTAGU INOCULATES HER SON AGAINST SMALLPOX.

Smallpox killed hundreds of thousands of people each year in the 18th century. But Turkish women came up with a solution that saved lives.

Lady Mary Wortley Montagu, the wife of Britain's ambassador to the Ottoman Empire, wrote home from Constantinople about the marvelous cure. Every September, older women would line up patients to inoculate them against smallpox by making a small cut on the patient and rubbing in a small amount of infectious material.

"The smallpox, so fatal, and so general amongst us, is here entirely harmless," Montagu marveled. She inoculated her own son, but London's physicians rejected the idea, refusing to believe that Turkish women might know more about medicine than trained doctors.

1723: ANTONIO VIVALDI COMPOSES THE FOUR SEASONS

Venetian composer Antonio Vivaldi wrote over forty operas. But today he is best known for his violin concertos called the Four Seasons.

Dedicating each concerto to one of the seasons of the year, Vivaldi drew on the scenic countryside of Mantua. The Four Seasons pushed musicians to recreate the sounds of birds in spring, the thunder of a rolling storm, and ice cracking on rivers.

Vivaldi didn't only write music to represent the Four Seasons. He also published sonnets to accompany each concerto.

Spring has arrived with joy
Welcomed by the birds with happy songs,
And the brooks, amidst gentle breezes,
Murmur sweetly as they flow.

1732: LAURA BASSI BECOMES THE FIRST FEMALE PROFESSOR.

At just 20 years old, Laura Bassi defended her doctoral dissertation in Bologna's town hall. She wrote on optics and light, becoming the first woman in history to earn a doctorate in science.

Bologna celebrated Bassi's achievements, publishing poems that lauded her brilliance. That same year, the University of Bologna invited

Bassi to become a professor of physics, making her the first female professor in history.

Although the university gave Bassi an official post, she was barred from teaching on campus because she was a woman. Instead, Bassi lectured students and conducted experiments from her home. She helped spread Newton's works to Italy and eventually became the chair of the university's experimental physics department.

1749: INFLUENTIAL FRENCH MATHEMATICIAN AND PHYSICIST EMILIE DU CHATELET DIES.

She was one of the greatest mathematicians in the 18th century. Emilie du Chatelet dedicated her studies to mathematics from a young age.

From the home she shared with Voltaire in the east of France, Emilie read and translated mathematical works by Leibniz and Newton. Her commentaries on Newton's work introduced the English scientist to generations of French students. Once, when a cafe kicked Emilie out for being a woman, she put on men's clothes and returned to debate with other intellectuals.

Emilie also published her own book on physics and translated Newton's *Principia Mathematica* into French. As Voltaire wrote after Emilie's death in childbirth, "she lived a life at a full tilt."

1751: THE FRENCH ENCYCLOPÉDIE ATTEMPTS TO CHRONICLE ALL KNOWLEDGE.

France's Enlightenment thinkers wanted to bring together all knowledge in one place. The *Encyclopédie* would encapsulate a secular approach to nature and the virtues of the Enlightenment.

Over three decades, a group of scholars created 35 volumes packed with everything an 18th-century scholar knew about science, nature, mathematics, manufacturing, and more. The *Encyclopédie* blended intellectual theory with the mechanical arts, detailing step by step how members of different trades practiced their arts.

Editor Denis Diderot said the project's goal was "to change the way people think." The *Encyclopédie* became a bold statement for reason in the face of blind faith laid the groundwork for the French Revolution.

1752: BENJAMIN FRANKLIN INVENTS THE LIGHTNING ROD

On the stormy night of June 10, 1752, Benjamin Franklin raced outside holding a kite and a metal key. Finally, Franklin would learn more about electricity. The dangerous experiment was the final step Franklin needed to prove that lightning was a form of electricity—and show the value of his new invention, the lightning rod.

That night, Franklin attached the key to his kite and flew it into a storm. Fortunately, lightning didn't actually strike Franklin's kite. Instead, the key attracted an electrical charge from the air and transferred it into a Leyden jar. The risky experiment proved Franklin right: lighting was electricity.

1754: BEN FRANKLIN PUBLISHES THE FIRST AMERICAN POLITICAL CARTOON.

"Join or Die," Benjamin Franklin's 1754 political cartoon warned. The image of a snake cut into pieces became a powerful symbol of colonial unity.

But the political cartoon wasn't created during the American Revolution, as many assume. Instead, Franklin published the image to convince the colonists to unite during the French and Indian War. If the colonies did not come together, Franklin believed, the French would overrun Britain's North American territories.

At the Albany Congress, Franklin called for a unified colonial government. A leader appointed by Britain would work with a council of colonial representatives to raise taxes and create military defenses. Although Franklin's plan failed in the 1750s, his political cartoon inspired revolutionaries a generation later.

1761: JOHN HARRISON CREATES A CLOCK ACCURATE ENOUGH TO CALCULATE LONGITUDE.

British sailors needed clocks. Without accurate watches, they could not calculate longitude at sea. In 1714, Parliament passed the Longitude Act, promising a massive monetary prize for anyone who could create a more accurate clock.

It took nearly half a century before someone claimed the prize. A self-taught clockmaker, John Harrison successfully created the most accurate timepiece in history. Known as H4, his fourth clock, Harrison spent years perfecting the device. In 1761, Harrison's watch went to sea, traveling from Britain to Jamaica. The timepiece was so impressive that the captain immediately placed an order for more watches.

The British initially refused to pay out the prize. Harrison didn't receive any compensation for his invention until he was 80 when the government paid out a fraction of the award.

1762: CATHERINE THE GREAT BECOMES EMPRESS OF RUSSIA.

Both a Prussian princess, Catherine the Great married into Russia's royalty. In 1744, she wed the grandson of Peter the Great. Both members of the unhappy union pursued affairs, and in 1762 Catherine's husband planned to set her aside.

Crafty Catherine staged a coup d'état against her own husband and became Russia's empress. For the next 34 years, Catherine ruled over Russia. As empress, Catherine expanded her empire's borders and pushed for reforms.

The British ambassador described Catherine as a ruler with "a masculine force of mine, obstinacy in adhering to a plan, and intrepidity in the execution of it"—high praise in the 18th century.

1770: MARIE ANTOINETTE MOVES TO PARIS TO MARRY THE HEIR TO THE FRENCH THRONE.

Marie Antoinette was the 15th child of Empress Maria Theresa. The powerful Austrian ruler saw her daughters as tools to seal alliances with rivals. In 1770, when her daughter had not yet turned fifteen, Maria Theresa sent Marie Antoinette to France, where she would marry the heir to the throne.

A massive entourage of nearly 60 carriages transported Marie Antoinette from Vienna to Paris, where she married the future Louis XVI. Before she turned 20, Marie Antoinette had become Queen of France.

The French found Marie Antoinette "more intelligent than has been generally supposed," but also criticized her as "rather lazy and extremely frivolous."

1773: THE BOSTON TEA PARTY PROTESTS BRITISH TAXES.

The Sons of Liberty dumped 45 tons of tea into Boston Harbor—worth nearly a million dollars in today's money. But what caused the Boston Tea Party?

By 1773, tensions between the American colonies and Great Britain had reached a boiling point. Colonists cried out against taxation without representation, demanding a voice in Parliament—or at least lower taxes.

The protest targeted tea for a good reason. Britain imposed steep taxes on tea, which many colonists resented. By destroying the tea and smuggling untaxed tea from other countries, the Americans resisted British rule.

Less than two years later, war broke out between the colonies and the British, leading to American independence.

1776: THE CONTINENTAL CONGRESS ADOPTS THE DECLARATION OF INDEPENDENCE.

"The second day of July 1776 will be the most memorable . . . in the history of America," John Adams declared.

Adams was right—but he was off by two days. All but one of the colonies approved the Declaration of Independence on July 2, 1776, but the Continental Congress did not officially adopt Thomas Jefferson's declaration until July 4th.

The Declaration of Independence publicly announced a break between the colonies and Great Britain. The colonies declared an independent, self-governing nation—though it would take years of war to truly win independence. America's founding document helped inspire the French Revolution thanks to its Enlightenment commitment to natural rights.

1778: JAMES COOK BECOMES THE FIRST EUROPEAN TO LAND ON THE HAWAIIAN ISLANDS.

Hawaii was the most remote place on the planet. In 1778, the English captain James Cook became the first European to visit the Hawaiian Islands, which he named the Sandwich Islands.

Cook had a long history of Pacific exploration. He'd visited Tahiti, New Zealand, and other South Pacific islands in the 1770s before crossing the Pacific and spotting Hawaii.

When Cook landed, the Hawaiians welcomed the crew. Cook traded iron to the Hawaiians, who saw the Europeans as god-like figures. But soon, the relationship between the explorers and the Hawaiians soured. When the Europeans proved mortal, the Hawaiians attacked Cook's party, angry at the crew's exploitation of their goodwill.

1781: WILLIAM HERSCHEL DISCOVERS URANUS, THE FIRST PLANET SPOTTED BY TELESCOPE.

The ancient astronomers knew about five planets—Mercury, Venus, Mars, Jupiter, and Saturn. But in 1781, astronomer William Herschel discovered a new planet by accident.

While scanning the skies with his 40-foot telescope, the largest in the world, Herschel noticed an object passing between the Earth and the stars. He eventually realized that he'd found another planet—the first to be spotted using a telescope.

Although Herschel wanted to name the planet for King George III, astronomers around the world refused such a British name. Instead, astronomers followed the pattern used to name ancient planets after Greek gods. As a result, the planet took the name Uranus.

1783: IN PARIS, THE FIRST PERSON RIDES IN A HOT AIR BALLOON.

Two French brothers created the first hot air balloon from silk and paper. In 1783, they demonstrated the invention in Paris, floating their unmanned balloon to over 5,000 feet of elevation.

The marvel quickly attracted attention from King Louis XVI. The inventors constructed a new balloon gilded in gold to impress the monarch. On Oct. 15, 1783, the brothers conducted their first manned balloon flight. But neither inventor wanted to board the balloon. Instead, they sent up a science teacher who became the first person to ride in a hot air balloon.

Benjamin Franklin, the U.S. ambassador to France, witnessed the first hot air balloon flight. "We observed it lift off in the most majestic manner," Franklin recorded, "We could not help feeling a certain mixture of awe and admiration."

1786: MOZART PREMIERES THE MARRIAGE OF FIGARO

The play had been banned in France and Vienna for attacking the aristocracy. But that didn't stop Wolfgang Amadeus Mozart from turning *The Marriage of Figaro* into an opera.

Mozart's opera showed crafty servants outsmarting their noble employers, raising eyebrows in the years directly before the French Revolution.

The Marriage of Figaro helped turn Mozart into a sensation on the opera scene. As he wrote to a friend, "Here they talk of nothing but *Figaro*. Nothing is played, sung or whistled but *Figaro*. No opera is drawing like *Figaro*. Nothing, nothing but *Figaro*." The composer went on to write *Don Giovanni*, *Cosi fan Tutti*, and the *Magic Flute*.

1789: ANTOINE LAVOISIER BECOMES THE "FATHER OF MODERN CHEMISTRY."

Antoine Lavoisier transformed chemistry into a modern science. He published the first chemistry textbook, classified the elements in the first periodic table, and named "oxygen."

Lavoisier, along with his wife Marie-Anne Paulze, conducted experiments to understand more about the elements. The couple designed instruments to perform experiments on respiration and published their findings.

But the man who earned the name "Father of Modern Chemistry" was also an aristocrat and tax collector who did not live through the French Revolution. A former tax collector, Lavoisier had pushed for reforms in the early years, but as the revolutionaries grew more radical he came under attack.

In 1794, Lavoisier was sent to the guillotine. As a fellow scientist wrote, "It took them only an instant to cut off that head, and a hundred years may not produce another like it."

1789: THE FRENCH STORM THE BASTILLE, STARTING THE FRENCH REVOLUTION.

Tensions between the French people and their rulers had brewed for generations. In 1789, after bread shortages and an extended economic crisis, Parisians turned against a symbol of royal power: the Bastille.

On July 14, 1789, an armed mob stormed the royal fortress, demanding the release of political prisoners. The governor of the Bastille quickly surrendered, allowing the Parisian crowd into the fortress. Inside, they seized gunpowder stores and cannons—while also releasing seven prisoners.

The fall of the Bastille symbolized the beginning of the French Revolution. France's old regime had officially fallen, and revolutionaries would remake the country. Over the next decade, France abolished the monarchy, executed their king and queen, and turned over power to Napoleon.

1790: THE FIRST U.S. CENSUS COUNTS AMERICA'S POPULATION.

The brand-new U.S. Constitution ordered Congress to carry out a census every ten years. The census would count everyone living in the states and territories of the new country—except for Native Americans, who were excluded until 1870, and slaves, who counted as 3/5ths of a person until the Civil War.

In 1790, the United States conducted its first census. Across the new nation, marshals visited every household on horseback to record information. The 1790 census counted every person, including free white males, free white females, other free persons, and slaves. When the final count came in, President George Washington learned that he governed over 3.9 million people.

1791: OLYMPE DE GOUGES WRITES THE DECLARATION ON THE RIGHTS OF WOMEN.

The French revolutionaries declared the rights of man in 1789, laying down the natural rights for citizens of France. In response, Olympe de Gouge wrote her own declaration on the rights of women.

Olympe de Gouges, a writer and activist, fought for women's rights and the abolition of slavery before the Revolution. She declared that women had a right to free speech, criticized the institution of marriage, and demanded a political role for women.

During the Reign of Terror, de Gouges was arrested and executed. "She wanted to be a man of state," one critic scoffed. "It seems the law has punished this conspirator for having forgotten the virtues that belong to her sex."

1791: THE HAITIAN REVOLUTION ESTABLISHES A NEW COUNTRY RUN BY FORMER SLAVES.

Inspired by the French Revolution's commitment to human rights, the slaves of France's wealthiest colony rebelled. In 1791, enslaved Haitians rose up against their masters, eventually creating a new state.

Led by Toussaint l'Overture, a former slave, the revolutionaries quickly expanded their control over the French colony of Saint-

Domingue. They even defeated French reinforcements and British invaders, eventually solidifying their position.

In 1801, the Haitians conquered the Dominican Republic, abolishing slavery and cementing their rule over the island of Hispaniola. Although Napoleon eventually captured l'Overture, his men successfully fought for their independence, becoming the nation of Haiti in 1804. Haiti became the first nation to permanently ban slavery and the slave trade.

1792: MARY WOLLSTONECRAFT PUBLISHES A VINDICATION OF THE RIGHTS OF WOMAN.

As 18th-century men fought for their natural rights, women joined the battle for women's rights. Abigail Adams reminded her Founding Father husband to "remember the ladies" when creating a new nation. And in England, Mary Wollstonecraft made a strong case for the rights of women.

Raised by an abusive father, Mary Wollstonecraft decided to earn her own living by opening a school. Based on her experience as a teacher, Wollstonecraft published a book on the importance of educating daughters and not just sons.

In 1792, Wollstonecraft wrote *A Vindication of the Rights of Women*, arguing that society treats women like "gentle domestic brutes." Wollstonecraft demanded educational reforms to treat women the same as men. With the benefits of an education, she argued, women could rival men in any area.

1796: EDWARD JENNER ADMINISTERS THE FIRST SMALLPOX VACCINATION.

Edward Jenner's first patient was just eight years old. In 1796, young James Phipps underwent an experimental treatment by an English surgeon who believed he could stop the deadly disease of smallpox. Jenner intentionally infected Phipps with cowpox to find out whether the milder disease protected children from smallpox.

The experiment worked. Jenner named the procedure after the Latin word for cow—vacca—terming his procedure a "vaccine."

At first, the British public refused to accept Jenner's evidence, even after he successfully vaccinated dozens more children, including his infant son. Critics ridiculed Jenner's vaccine, calling it dangerous. But Jenner's vaccine won out—soon, patients around the world lined up for history's first vaccine.

1799: NAPOLEON'S TROOPS DISCOVER THE ROSETTA STONE IN EGYPT.

For three years, Napoleon's troops marched through Egypt. And in 1799 they made a surprising discovery—a black stone that held the secret to a centuries-old mystery.

The French soldiers found the stone while digging the foundation for a new fort. After unearthing the Rosetta Stone, they noticed three scripts carved into the rock—Greek, demotic Egyptian, and Egyptian hieroglyphs. It was a startling discovery since no one had used hieroglyphs since the 300s, and not even scholars could read them.

For years, no one could decode the languages on the Rosetta Stone. In the early 19th century, British and French scholars painstakingly decoded the hieroglyphs, unlocking a new tool to understand the ancient Egyptians.

THE INDUSTRIAL ERA (1800S)

1805: LEWIS AND CLARK REACH THE PACIFIC OCEAN.

On Nov. 15, 1805, the men of Lewis and Clark's expedition finally reached the Pacific Ocean. The journey from St. Louis had taken over 18 grueling months as the party crossed the Rocky Mountains on foot.

The exhausted members of the expedition had just spent several days sheltering in a "dismal nitch" as rains battered the coast. For six days, the men waited for the rains to stop. Then, after reaching the mouth of the Columbia, the party voted to set up winter quarters on the south shore before returning overland to Missouri.

Lewis and Clark failed to find the fabled Northwest Passage connecting the Missouri River with the Columbia River. But their expedition successfully mapped the geography of the West, building alliances with several important Native American tribes.

1810: CORNELIUS VANDERBILT STARTS HIS FIRST BUSINESS

He became one of the most powerful railroad barons in history. When Cornelius Vanderbilt started his first business in 1810, he was still a teenager. At just 16 years old, Vanderbilt began ferrying people across the Hudson River, bringing in $1,000 in his first year of business.

Before his 20th birthday, Vanderbilt controlled a fleet of boats, transporting freight and passengers up and down the eastern seaboard. During the Civil War, he donated a ship to the Union and retired from the shipping business.

But Vanderbilt didn't give up on business. Instead, he moved into railroads, building an empire that transformed Vanderbilt into the richest man in the U.S.

1812: IN ENGLAND, THE LUDDITES BEGIN TO SMASH NEW MACHINES.

Technology was putting Englishmen out of a job, the Luddites declared in 1812. A movement of weavers and textile workers, the Luddites lashed out at the mechanized tools replacing their labor.

In 1812, Luddites organized to break machines across the English countryside. They raided and burned factories to disrupt production. The Luddites hoped to convince business owners to stop buying the machines. Instead, the Luddites triggered a strong response from the British government, which saw industrialization as key to their empire's strength. The government made machine breaking a capital offense, even deploying the army to arrest and hang Luddites.

Although their movement failed, the Luddites brought attention to the potential downsides of industrialization.

1813: JANE AUSTEN PUBLISHES PRIDE AND PREJUDICE

As a young girl, Jane Austen scribbled stories in notebooks. As an adult, Austen became one of the most celebrated female authors of all time.

In her 20s, as she balanced an active social life with her hidden pursuit of writing, Austen began to write a book she called *First Impressions*. The novel was her "darling child," Austen wrote. In 1813 she published the book as *Pride and Prejudice*.

When Austen published her first novel, *Sense and Sensibility*, she did not want to attach her name to her work. Instead, she labeled the book 'By a Lady'. In *Pride and Prejudice*, Austen identified herself as 'the Author of *Sense and Sensibility*." At the time, publishing was not seen as a "lady-like" occupation.

1813: CANADIAN LAURA SECORD WALKS 20 MILES TO WARN OF A SURPRISE ATTACK BY THE U.S.

Laura Secord crossed 20 miles "to save the British troops from capture or perhaps total destruction."

During the War of 1812, the U.S. invaded Canada. Secord, caring for a wounded husband, learned of a U.S. attack against a British storehouse. To warn the British, Secord set off across the countryside and through a swamp, avoiding American soldiers who patrolled the roads. Teaming up with a group of Native warriors, Secord reached the British and foiled the attack.

It wasn't the first time Laura's family sided with the British. The family once lived in Massachusetts but moved to Canada during the American Revolution. Canadians celebrate Secord for her journey, which helped the British push the Americans out of Canada.

1814: LONDON HOLDS ITS LAST FROST FAIR ON THE FROZEN THAMES RIVER.

For centuries, the Thames River in London froze solid. In the coldest winters, Londoners would meet on the ice to hold frost fairs.

The practice started out of necessity. When the Thames froze, it left London without its main source of trade. The frost fairs gave the city's watermen a new source of income. They could charge traders to set up stalls on the ice.

In 1814, London held its last frost fair. Visitors bought drinks and roasted oxen. Printing presses handed out slips of paper as souvenirs. And Londoners danced as an elephant marched across the ice.

For days, Londoners drank hot chocolate and ate mince pies. But when the ice melted, the frost fairs ended—the Thames never again froze thick enough to hold a fair.

1818: MARY SHELLEY PUBLISHES FRANKENSTEIN

She was the daughter of Mary Wollstonecraft, but instead of writing about women's rights, Mary Shelley wrote about the power of science to manipulate nature. In her most famous book, *Frankenstein*, Shelley

In 1816, Shelley spent the summer in Switzerland with her husband and Lord Byron. One night, Lord Byron challenged each member of their group to write a ghost story. Mary sat down and penned a draft of *Frankenstein*. The idea came to Shelley during a thunderstorm. "I saw the hideous phantasm of a man stretched out," she later wrote, "and then, on the working of some powerful engine, show signs of life."

Two years later, Shelley rocked the literary world by publishing her novel anonymously. Most readers attributed the work to her husband, Percy Bysshe Shelley.

1825: THE ERIE CANAL CONNECTS THE GREAT LAKES TO THE ATLANTIC OCEAN.

Nearly 400 miles of land separated the Great Lakes from the Hudson River. In 1825, after eight years of work, a parade of boats sailed down the new Erie Canal, a 363-mile channel carved into the earth. If explorers couldn't find a water route to link the fertile Midwest to the East Coast, Americans would build their own.

Originally, the canal stood at just four feet deep. Traveling the Erie Canal meant going up and down 83 locks. But the canal made it much easier to ship wheat and corn to the east or furniture to the west.

The cost of transporting goods from the frontier was slashed to only a tenth of the previous cost. Within three decades, the Erie Canal accounted for over 60% of all U.S. trade.

1842: DOCTORS USE ANESTHESIA FOR THE FIRST TIME.

In the 1840s, doctors began using anesthesia for the first time. Patients undergoing surgery, women giving birth, and people having a tooth pulled finally had better pain relief options.

The American doctor William Morton personally took part in safety experiments, buying ether and inhaling the fumes to test their reliability.

When Morton decided ether was safe, he started treating his dental patients with anesthesia. And ether wasn't the only anesthesia. Morton also tested laughing gas on patients.

Another surgeon, John Collins Warren, declared, "Gentlemen, this is no humbug." Queen Victoria became the first monarch to give birth with anesthesia in 1853 when John Snow administered chloroform during the birth of her eighth child.

1843: THE FIRST WAGON TRAIN TRAVELS WEST FROM MISSOURI ON THE OREGON TRAIL.

Settlers on the Oregon Trail followed the Platte River to Wyoming, where they crossed the Rocky Mountains and trailed the Columbia River to Oregon Territory.

In 1843, the first major wagon train left Elm Grove, Missouri to travel west. The group of a thousand people, divided into 100 wagons, brought along a massive herd of 5,000 cattle.

Small groups of settlers had traveled west on routes charted by fur traders before 1843. But soon, thousands traveled the Oregon Trail every year, hoping for a better life in the west. An economic depression had made life even harder in the Midwest, driving many to seek a better life on the West Coast.

1847: THE BRONTË SISTERS PUBLISH JANE EYRE AND WUTHERING HEIGHTS.

Charlotte, Emily, and Anne Brontë began writing stories as children. After spending years working as governesses and teachers, the sisters finally decided to publish their stories under male pseudonyms.

Between 1847 and 1848, the sisters published *Jane Eyre*, *Wuthering Heights*, *Agnes Grey*, and *The Tenant* using the last name Bell. *Jane Eyre* instantly became a best-seller, though *Wuthering Heights* did not. Even their publisher didn't realize the sisters had written the books, until one day "rather quaintly dressed little ladies, pale-faced and anxious-looking" showed up in his office.

But by 1849, both Emily and Anne had died from tuberculosis.

Charlotte, the last surviving member of her family, also succumbed to the disease in 1855.

1848: THE DISCOVERY OF GOLD IN CALIFORNIA CREATES A GOLD RUSH.

On Jan. 24, 1848, James Marshall pulled something shiny from a creek in the foothills of the Sierra Nevadas. By finding gold at Sutter's Mill, Marshall kicked off a gold rush that would bring 100,000 people to California.

As tales of gold nuggets plucked from rivers reached the east, prospectors flooded west. In 1849, the "Forty-Niners" swarmed to California, seeking gold. Some struck it rich, while many others opened saloons and stores to cater to the Forty-Niners. The Gold Rush transformed San Francisco from a minor village to a major American city, increasing its population by 25 times in two years.

California's swelling population and the promise of riches pushed the United States to make the territory a state in 1850.

1849: AUSTRIA SENDS 200 BALLOONS TO DROP BOMBS ON VENICE.

The first air raid in history didn't happen in World War I—it didn't even happen in the 20th century. In 1849, Austria used hot air balloons to drop bombs on Venice during a siege.

The Austrians decided to attach bombs to balloons in July 1849. An artillery officer came up with the idea, counting on the wind to drift the balloons over the floating city. A timer made from cotton thread and charcoal would drop the bomb once it reached Venice. But the first attempt completely failed, with some balloons floating over Austria's forces.

The Austrians tried again in August, sending 30 pounds of explosives floating on 200 balloons. Although a few landed in the city, they didn't cause much damage—but the first air raid marked a change in warfare.

1850: HARRIET TUBMAN MAKES HER FIRST JOURNEY INTO THE SOUTH TO BRING SLAVES TO FREEDOM.

Born into slavery, Harriet Tubman risked her life multiple times to help other enslaved people make the journey to freedom on the Underground Railroad. From 1850-1860, Tubman traveled the Underground Railroad 19 times, leading over 300 people to freedom.

Harriet knew the route well because she'd used the Underground Railroad to escape slavery in 1849. "When I found I had crossed that line," Harriet said about reaching freedom in Philadelphia, "I looked at my hands to see if I was the same person. There was such a glory over everything; the sun came like gold through the trees, and over the fields, and I felt like I was in Heaven."

During the Civil War, Tubman signed up as a spy for the Union, sneaking into Confederate territory to report. In the Combahee River Raid, Tubman helped liberate over 700 people.

1851: SOJOURNER TRUTH DELIVERS THE SPEECH "AIN'T I A WOMAN?"

"I did not run away, I walked away by daylight," Sojourner Truth told her slave owner. In 1951, Truth attended the Women's Rights Convention in Ohio and gave an influential speech. In her "Ain't I a Woman?" Truth linked women's rights with the abolition of slavery, pushing white activists to recognize the humanity of enslaved women.

Sojourner questioned whether the Victorian ideal of femininity included Black women, saying, "Look at me! Look at my arm! I have ploughed and planted, and gathered into barns, and no man could head me! And ain't I a woman? I could work as much and eat as much as a man - when I could get it - and bear the lash as well! And ain't I a woman?"

1852: HARRIET BEECHER STOWE PUBLISHES UNCLE TOM'S CABIN.

Slavery was a brutal institution that tore families apart. In 1852, Harriet Beecher Stowe's novel *Uncle Tom's Cabin* became an instant bestseller thanks to its emotional attack on slavery. One newspaper reported,

"Never since books were first printed has the success of Uncle Tom been equaled."

An abolitionist, Stowe drew on slave narratives and her own pain at the death of her young son to capture the horrors of slavery. The novel inspired such strong feelings that owning a copy became illegal in the South—one man even went to jail for owning *Uncle Tom's Cabin.*

During the Civil War, Stowe visited President Abraham Lincoln in Washington, D.C. The president remarked, "So you are the little woman who wrote the book that started this great war."

1854: IN LONDON, CONSTRUCTION ENDS ON BIG BEN.

In 1834, the Palace of Westminster burned. To replace it, architects designed a massive clock tower that became known as Big Ben.

In fact, the tower itself isn't called Big Ben—that's the name of the largest bell inside. Big Ben was so large that it actually cracked in 1859. The massive town incorporates Yorkshire stone and Cornish granite, while the iron came from Birmingham. The clock measured the largest in the world for decades, with the minute hand stretching 14 feet long.

German bombing raids nearly destroyed Big Ben in 1941, and in 2017, Britain renamed the clock tower after Queen Elizabeth II as part of her Diamond Jubilee, celebrating 60 years as queen.

1854: JOHN SNOW STOPS A CHOLERA OUTBREAK BY PROVING THE DISEASE IS WATERBORNE.

Cholera struck down millions of victims in the 19th century. But in 1854, an English physician traced a brewing outbreak to the Broad Street Pump, potentially saving thousands of lives.

Who was John Snow? A doctor from York, Snow proved that cholera spread through water. Most doctors believed "bad air," or miasma, spread disease. Even before germ theory, Snow showed how people who drank from the Broad Street Pump came down with cholera, convincing the city to remove the pump handle.

Snow's pioneering work helped convince cities to invest in public health improvements. In London, water companies stopped pumping water from downriver, where waste contaminated the water.

1859: THE FIRST RABBIT ARRIVES IN AUSTRALIA

European settlers wanted something to hunt in Australia. So in 1859, a wealthy British settler released 13 European wild rabbits on his estate to hunt for sport.

The decision quickly became an ecological disaster. Within years, the rabbit population escaped the estate. Australians put up 200,000 miles of fences to contain the rabbits. But by the early 20th century, rabbits had spread across the continent, destroying indigenous plants and animals.

In the late 1940s, the continent counted 600 million rabbits, undeterred by fences and other attempts to control their population. Today, at least 150 million rabbits live in Australia.

1859: CHARLES DARWIN PUBLISHES ON THE ORIGIN OF SPECIES.

How did plants and animals change over time? British naturalist Charles Darwin presented his answer in *On the Origin of Species*: natural selection.

On a journey to the Galapagos Islands, a young Darwin observed finches adapted perfectly to the island's food sources. By studying fossils, the scientist tracked changes in species. Darwin began to suspect that the animals most adapted to their environments survived, which he termed natural selection.

Darwin wasn't the first to suggest that species evolved over time. But he provided an evidence-based argument for what drove those changes. Darwin's mechanism to explain evolution struck a chord. The book quickly became a bestseller and shaped science for generations.

1861: DETECTIVE KATE WARNE FOILS AN ASSASSINATION ATTEMPT AGAINST ABRAHAM LINCOLN.

She was the first private female detective in history. And in 1861, Kate Warne saved President Abraham Lincoln's life.

Warne joined the Pinkerton Detective Agency in the 1850s. As founder Allan Pinkerton wrote, "She could go and worm out secrets in many places which it was impossible for male detectives to gain access." Warne proved that in 1861 when she disguised herself as Lincoln's sister to protect the president's life.

Southern conspirators wanted to assassinate the president. But with an undercover Warne at his side on a whistle-stop tour of Baltimore, Lincoln survived the plot and led the Union to victory in the Civil War.

1863: THE FIRST SECTION OF THE LONDON UNDERGROUND OPENS.

It was the world's first underground railway—and in 1863, the London Underground opened for business.

London's first underground system connected Paddington with Farringdon Street. On opening day, 38,000 passengers flocked to the underground railway to ride the rails. Operated by the Metropolitan Railway, the 3.75-mile line soon carried passengers on steam trains. Passengers climbed into wooden carriage lit with gas lanterns, and steam locomotives carried them through the tunnels.

But when trains traveled under the River Thames in the famous Thames Tunnel, passengers had to practically hold their breath—there was no ventilation system to vent the smoke. Fortunately, by 1913 the railway switched to electric trains.

1864: LOUIS PASTEUR INVENTS THE PASTEURIZATION PROCESS

For centuries, scientists believed in spontaneous generation. Until French scientist Louis Pasteur conducted experiments that proved meat broth couldn't spontaneously grow life. Along the way, Pasteur invented a process to remove bacteria from beverages: pasteurization.

In his experiments, Pasteur boiled meat broth and isolated it from the air. No bacteria grew in the broth, showing Pasteur the power of sterilization. Soon, Pasteur realized that microorganisms soured beer and milk. Thanks to that research, Pasteur came up with a process to eliminate bacteria from milk. After boiling the milk to kill bacteria, dairy producers would cool the milk to sell it. Over a century later, dairy farmers still rely on pasteurization to make milk safer.

1865: GREGOR MENDEL'S RESEARCH ON PEA PLANTS PIONEERS THE FIELD OF GENETICS.

An Austrian monk spent years growing pea plants from his remote monastery. Although his work went unrecognized during his lifetime, Gregor Mendel pioneered the field of genetics through his study of heredity.

In the monastery's garden, Mendel crossed different types of pea plants. Would their offspring have smooth or wrinkled peas? Would the stems grow tall or short? Would their flowers grow purple or white? By charting the outcomes, Mendel showed that plants passed on traits at a distinct ratio.

A generation later, the new field of genetics unearthed a single paper Mendel published in a Czech journal and realized the monk had decoded heredity.

1865: MARY EDWARD WALKER BECOMES THE ONLY WOMAN TO WIN THE MEDAL OF HONOR.

She was the only female surgeon during the Civil War. But when Mary Edwards Walker crossed enemy lines to care for civilians, the Confederacy captured her, accused her of spying, and threw Walker in prison.

Walker fought for her spot in the Union Army. After the Union rejected her as a medical officer, Walker became an unpaid volunteer surgeon and later convinced the army to give her a commission in Ohio. After the war, she also fought for recognition from President Andrew Johnson, who finally agreed to award Walker the Medal of Honor.

Walker continued to fight long after the Civil War—she was arrested for wearing pants and fought for women's right to vote.

1866: TRANSATLANTIC TELEGRAPH CABLES CONNECT THE U.S. AND UK.

On Aug. 16, 1858, Queen Victoria sent a message to President James Buchanan. Instead of taking weeks to cross the ocean by steamship, the message traveled almost instantaneously on the new transatlantic telegraph.

The effort to create a permanent telegraph cable linking Europe and North America took over a decade. Cyrus West Field sent dozens of ships across the Atlantic, trying to lay down an unbroken insulated line. But time after time, the effort failed. The cable would need to stretch 2,000 miles at a depth of up to two miles.

Although West linked the UK and the U.S. in 1858, it proved short lived—within weeks, the cable failed. West quickly raised more funds, finally laying the first permanent telegraph line in 1866. After speeding up communications between Europe and the U.S., West turned to laying telegraph lines in the Pacific.

1869: THE TRANSCONTINENTAL RAILROAD CROSSES THE U.S

Every year, thousands of settlers moved west in covered wagons. But the new transcontinental railroad changed everything.

On May 10, 1869, a crowd met just north of the Great Salt Lake to link lines built by the Central Pacific and Union Pacific. The final spike joining the two lines and connecting the East Coast with the West was made from solid gold.

Chinese immigrants, Irish immigrants, and Civil War veterans helped build the railroad, often working under dangerous conditions. Workers blasted through mountains with gunpowder and raced to meet impossible deadlines. Once the transcontinental railroad opened, travelers could cross the continent in a few days instead of the months required in a wagon.

1872: THE U.S. CREATES ITS FIRST NATIONAL PARK: YELLOWSTONE.

In 1872, Congress passed a bill to turn Yellowstone into the country's first national park. Thanks to photographs, paintings, and sketches of the park, Congressmen who had never visited the West saw the value in preserving the area. In the Yellowstone National Park Protection Act, Congress declared Yellowstone "a public park or pleasuring-ground for the benefit and enjoyment of the people."

Managing the new national park created some administrative challenges. In the early 20th century, Congress created the National Park Service to manage Yellowstone and other parks like Yosemite, Sequoia, Mount Rainier, the Grand Canyon, and Mesa Verde. Today, over 330 million visitors enjoy the country's national parks each year.

1876: ROBERT KOCH DEVELOPS A PROCEDURE TO PROVE THE GERM THEORY OF DISEASE.

Were diseases caused by bad air or something else? In 1876, the German doctor Robert Koch proved that germs caused diseases, ushering in a new era of medicine.

Koch learned about germs by experimenting with a deadly bacteria called anthrax. He examined blood samples from cows that died from anthrax, identifying a microscopic bacteria with the potential to spread the disease. Koch then infected mice with anthrax-laced blood, showing that the mice came down with the disease.

After identifying the cause of anthrax, Koch went on to discover the bacteria that caused tuberculosis and cholera, major killers in the 19th century. Koch became one of the first scientists to win a Nobel Prize.

1885: LOUIS PASTEUR CREATES THE FIRST SUCCESSFUL VACCINE AGAINST RABIES.

Louis Pasteur believed in the germ theory of disease—and quickly realized that germ theory opened the door to new possibilities with vaccines.

In the 1880s, Pasteur began researching vaccines in his laboratory, where he discovered how to weaken germs to create safer vaccines. Thanks to his technique, Pasteur create a vaccine that protected chickens from cholera and another that protected sheep from anthrax.

After mastering animal vaccines, the scientist turned to a vaccine against rabies. But creating a vaccine for humans posed ethical problems. Still, in 1885, Pasteur successfully tested the first rabies vaccine on a nine-year-old boy exposed to the disease. Without the vaccine, the boy would have almost certainly died—but the vaccine saved his life.

1885: JOHN PEMBERTON PATENTS COCA-COLA, A DRINK OF COCAINE, COLA NUTS, AND CITRUS.

He was a biochemist who fought for the Confederacy. And in 1885, John Pemberton created a new beverage: Coca-Cola.

Originally sold as Pemberton's French Wine Coca, the drink packed a punch. It contained alcohol, cocaine-laced coca leaves, and caffeine-packed kola nuts. Pemberton marketed the soda as a headache remedy and mental aid, claiming it could calm the nerves.

Just one year later, Pemberton removed the alcohol from his drink and added citric acid. In its first year, Coca-Cola only brought in $50, but a century later sales reached into the billions—though without the coca leaves, which were removed in the early 20th century.

1889: IN PARIS, THE EIFFEL TOWER IS INAUGURATED.

The Eiffel Tower celebrated the 100th anniversary of the French Revolution. On Mar. 31, 1889, 200 construction workers lined up before the tower to watch its inauguration. The ceremony celebrated the world's tallest man-made tower, which let visitors gaze across all of Paris from over 900 feet in the air.

During the inauguration, Parisians watched as the French flag waved atop the tower and fireworks burst from the second platform.

Although critics worried the iron tower would embarrass the city, the Eiffel Tower quickly became a symbol of Paris. It remained the tallest man-man structure until 1930 when New York's Chrysler Building took the crown.

1891: LILIUOKALANI BECOMES THE FIRST QUEEN OF HAWAII.

She was Hawaii's first and last queen. In 1891, Liliuokalani became the Queen of Hawaii when her brother died. But after only two years of rule, a military coup removed Liliuokalani from power.

Queen Liliuokalani fought for the rights of native Hawaiians against wealthy Western landowners who owned sugar plantations on the islands. After pushing for a new constitution, the landowners seized power and reached out to the U.S., which agreed to annex Hawaii. When Liliuokalani led a revolt, the new government arrested the former queen and charged her with treason.

Liliuokalani spent the rest of her life fighting against Hawaii's annexation and pushing for the restoration of the monarchy.

1896: IN ATHENS, THE OLYMPIC GAMES ARE REVIVED.

It had been 1,500 years since the Greeks held the Olympic Games. But in 1896, Athens revived the Olympic Games, welcoming athletes representing 13 different nations.

To honor the history of the games, many events took place in an ancient Greek stadium built in 330 BCE.

What events did the first modern Olympic Games include? Favorites like track and field, gymnastics, wrestling, and swimming made the cut. So did newer sports like tennis. Like the ancient Olympic Games, only men competed in 1896. But by the second Olympic Games in 1900, held in Paris, women competed and won medals in fencing and sailing.

THE MODERN WORLD (1900S-TODAY)

1900: PROHIBITIONIST CARRY NATION SMASHES SALOONS WITH A HATCHET.

In the early 20th century. Prohibitionists fought to ban alcohol sales in the U.S. One even visited bars and smashed them with her hatchet.

Carry Nation landed herself in jail after she caused thousands of dollars in damage at a Kansas bar. A member of the Women's Christian Temperance Union, Nation's first husband died from alcoholism.

Nation traveled the country to speak out against alcohol. She became known for carrying a hatchet and even sold souvenir hatchets to her many followers.

Although Carry Nation died before Prohibition banned alcohol in every state, she played a major role in pushing for temperance.

1903: MARIE CURIE WINS HER FIRST (OF TWO) NOBEL PRIZE.

In 1903, Marie Curie became the first woman to win a Nobel Prize. Born in Poland, Marie mastered physics and chemistry, discovering the elements polonium and radium. Curie's research into uranium pioneered the field of atomic physics. Marie came up with the name "radioactivity," the research that won her a Nobel Prize.

The Nobel Prize helped fund Curie's research. The prize money helped Curie invest in a lab to learn more about atomic physics. Later in her life, Curie won a second Nobel Prize in chemistry, making her the first person to win two Nobel Prizes in different fields. She also developed x-rays and continued her research into radioactivity.

1903: THE INVENTION OF THE TEDDY BEAR, NAMED FOR PRESIDENT TEDDY ROOSEVELT.

The teddy bear didn't exist until the 20th century. Early in his first presidential term, Theodore Roosevelt visited Mississippi to hunt for bears. After he didn't sight a single creature, one of the president's assistants tied a black bear to a willow tree. Roosevelt refused, deeming it unsportsmanlike to shoot the bear.

The president's encounter with the bear soon made headlines across the country. One political cartoonist drew the scene. When a Brooklyn toy store owner saw the cartoon, he created a stuffed animal based on the story and sent it to the president. Roosevelt approved of the teddy bear, and the teddy bear became one of the most famous toys in history.

1903: THE WRIGHT BROTHERS MAKE THE FIRST FLIGHT IN A POWERED AIRPLANE.

"It is possible to fly without motors, but not without knowledge and skill," Wilbur Wright said. That philosophy convinced the Wright brothers to build manned planes guided by pilots,

The brothers started by sailing their glider from a hill in North Carolina, where they built flying skills before adding a motor to their design. Only then did the brothers add a gasoline engine to their propeller plane.

The 600-pound flyer made its first successful flight on Dec. 17, 1903, traveling 120 feet at a pace of under 7 mph. But by the end of the day, the brothers kept their plane afloat for over 850 feet. The brothers rushed to send their father a telegram reporting on their achievement.

1903: THE FIRST TOUR DE FRANCE TAKES PLACE.

On the afternoon of July 1, 1903, 60 cyclists took off from Paris on the first Tour de France. The 1,500-mile loop around France became an annual tradition, but the first day of the first Tour de France nearly destroyed the race.

On the first day, riders were told to cover 300 miles. The cyclists zipped down unpaved roads, without support cars or even helmets. As the sun set on the first day, the riders were forced to ride through the night lit only by the moon. After the first day, 23 riders quit.

At the end of the race, Maurice Garin sped into Paris, cheered by 20,000 spectators. Only 21 of the original 60 riders finished the race. But the Tour de France became a media sensation and the tradition continued.

1904: HELEN KELLER GRADUATES FROM RADCLIFFE COLLEGE

An illness left Helen Keller blind and deaf as a toddler. But in 1887, Anne Sullivan helped Keller regain her ability to communicate, and a decade later Keller was ready to go off to college.

But college wasn't an easy journey. First, Keller had to win over a patron. Keller met and impressed the writer Mark Twain, who introduced her to Henry H. Rogers, who worked for Standard Oil. Rogers offered to pay for Keller to attend college.

After graduating from preparatory schools for the deaf in Boston and New York City, Keller enrolled at Radcliffe College, the sister school to Harvard. Sullivan attended classes with Keller to help her interpret lectures and readings. In 1904, Keller earned her bachelor of arts degree, becoming the first person with deafblindness to graduate from college.

1905: ALBERT EINSTEIN FORMULATES RELATIVITY

A German physicist overturned centuries of scientific theories with his theory of relativity. Albert Einstein, born in Germany, dedicated his "miracle year" to studying light and electrodynamics. In the same year that the posited $E=MC^2$, Einstein also proposed a theory of relativity that upended Newtonian physics.

Observations, Einstein claimed, depended on the observer's motion. Light, gravity, space, and time itself could also influence observations. Thanks to Einstein's theories, physicists could more accurately predict planetary orbits and understand gravity much more precisely. At first, other physicists rejected Einstein's work—until observations backed his predictions. The theory of relativity would earn Einstein a spot among the greatest scientists in history.

1908: THE FIRST MODEL T FORD APPEARS IN DETROIT.

The first Model T rolled off the production line at the Ford Motor Company in 1908. It wasn't the first car, but the Model T became one of the most influential cars in history.

That's because Henry Ford intentionally set an affordable price for the Model T—just $850. Although the car cost slightly more than the average worker's income, it was affordable enough that a majority of Americans eventually owned the car. Ford didn't bother to offer many customization options on his car. As he quipped, "Any customer can have a car painted any color that he wants so long as it is black."

Between 1913-1927, Ford churned out 15 million Model Ts.

1911: ROALD AMUNDSEN REACHES THE SOUTH POLE

The race to the South Pole ended when a Norwegian expedition led by Roald Amundsen reached the South Pole in 1911.

Amundsen raced against the British explorer Robert Scott. While Amundsen's team used skis and sled dogs, Scott tried to cross the continent with ponies and tractors. After machines broke and the ponies died, Scott's men had to pull their own supplies.

On Dec. 14, 1911, Amundsen reached the South Pole. "The goal was reached," Amundsen declared, "our journey ended"—except for the treacherous trip back to his base camp. A month later, Scott also reached the goal. "Great God!" Scott recorded in his diary. "This is an awful place and terrible enough for us to have labored to it without the reward of priority." Scott and his men died on the return journey.

1911: LEONARDO DA VINCI'S MONA LISA IS STOLEN FROM THE LOUVRE IN PARIS.

It was one of the greatest thefts in art history. In 1911, someone broke into the Louvre and stole the *Mona Lisa*. For two years, the police tracked down suspects, including Pablo Picasso, and a media firestorm raged. Who had stolen da Vinci's masterpiece?

The mystery continued until 1913 when police finally caught Vincenzo Perugia. The art thief had snuck into the gallery dressed as an employee and hidden until closing time to snatch the painting. When the Louvre reopened the next day, Perugia simply walked out the door with the *Mona Lisa* hidden under his uniform.

Perugia defended himself by claiming that the conqueror Napoleon had stolen the painting, which rightfully belonged in Italy. But the police returned the painting to the Louvre and sent Perugia to jail.

1912: HENRIETTA SWAN LEAVITT UNCOVERS THE SIZE OF THE UNIVERSE.

The Harvard College Observatory hired women as "calculators" to run complex calculations in the days before computers. One of those women, Henrietta Swan Leavitt, discovered over 2,400 stars during her time working at Harvard.

A graduate of Radcliffe College, Leavitt worked for seven years at the observatory before director Charles Pickering hired her at 30 cents an hour. Leavitt measured the magnitude of stars using photographs, specializing in the variable stars that change luminosity. Thanks to her observations, Leavitt discovered a connection between the brightness cycle and the star's distance—data that later allowed Edwin Hubble to measure the size of the universe.

1920: WOMEN GAIN THE RIGHT TO VOTE IN THE U.S.

For nearly a century, women in the U.S. marched and organized for voting rights. In 1920, the 19th Amendment finally gave women the right to vote.

Passing the 19th Amendment wasn't easy. In Tennessee, the final state to tip the balance toward ratification, the state legislator tied the vote, leaving a 23-year-old representative to break the tie. Harry T. Burns personally opposed women's suffrage, but his mother convinced him to vote in favor of the amendment.

Although the Constitution now gave all men and women the right to vote, many states continued to block Black voters until after the Civil Rights movement.

1927: ZOOLOGIST KARL VON FRISCH SHOWS THAT BEES COMMUNICATE THROUGH DANCE.

In the 1920s, zoologist Karl von Frisch noticed something unusual about honey bees. When one bee found a feeding station in his lab, others quickly appeared in the same location. Were the bees communicating with each other?

Von Frisch discovered that honey bees communicate through a special dance language. One dance, called the round dance, told other bees to look for food nearby. The more complicated waggle dance told bees which direction to fly and how far. Scout bees use the straight lines of the honeycomb inside the hive to orient their dance, orienting the other bees based on the sun's location. Thanks to his patience, von Frisch unlocked the secret of the honey bee dance.

1928: ALEXANDER FLEMING ACCIDENTALLY DISCOVERS PENICILLIN

One summer, Alexander Fleming left his lab in London to vacation in Scotland. When he returned in September, Fleming found something growing on his Petri dishes. Fleming had accidentally discovered penicillin, the most important antibiotic in history.

After noticing the mold growing on his Petri dishes, Fleming realized the fungus *Penicillium notatum* stopped the growth of bacteria. Fleming quickly realized the fungus could be used to fight deadly diseases.

"When I woke up just after dawn on September 28, 1928, I certainly didn't plan to revolutionize all medicine by discovering the world's first antibiotic, or bacteria killer," Fleming later wrote. "But I guess that was exactly what I did."

1930: A SYRIAN HAMSTER BECOMES THE ANCESTOR OF EVERY PET HAMSTER IN THE WORLD.

Today, hamsters rank as one of the most popular pets in the U.S. And every pet hamster can trace its ancestry back to a Syrian hamster from Syria.

In 1930, scientists caught a wild hamster and her litter in Syria. The hamsters would participate in a behavioral study in Jerusalem. But the lab workers in Jerusalem quickly fell for the hamsters, taking some home as pets. Those same lab workers shipped descendants of the original hamster family to labs in other countries.

Over the next decade, people around the world domesticated the hamster, making it a popular pet from the 1940s on.

1933: PROHIBITION ENDS IN THE UNITED STATES

The American experiment with Prohibition ended in 1933 after over a decade of outlawing alcohol. During the era of Prohibition, bootleggers like Al Capone flourished and organized crime skyrocketed.

The temperance movement pushed for a national ban on alcohol for decades before it finally went into effect in 1920. Federal agents tracked down bootleggers and poured out thousands of barrels of booze. Alcohol consumption went underground, with speakeasies springing up across the country. By the early 1930s, many saw Prohibition as a failure—and an expensive one, since the federal government gave up billions in tax revenue by outlawing booze. The 21st Amendment repealed Prohibition in 1933.

But Prohibition didn't end everywhere. Some states continued to ban alcohol. The last dry state—Mississippi—only ended Prohibition in 1966.

1939: THE WIZARD OF OZ FLOPS, AND LATER BECOMES A CLASSIC.

When *The Wizard of Oz* hit theaters in 1939, it lost money. The lush color film cost $3 million to make, but theatergoers paid only a dime or quarter to see the movie. Yet today, *The Wizard of Oz* is the most-watched movie in history. How did *The Wizard of Oz* go from a flop to a classic?

In the Golden Age of Hollywood, movies premiered in theaters and then seemingly vanished. With no way to watch movies at home, the initial theater run represented the only chance to see a film—and the only chance for studios to make a profit.

Until 1956, when CBS decided to air *The Wizard of Oz* on television. A stunning 45 million viewers tuned in, and the airing became an annual tradition—helping transform the flop into a classic.

1941: ORSON WELLES WRITES, DIRECTS, AND STARS IN CITIZEN KANE.

When a young Orson Welles decided to base a movie on the media mogul William Randolph Hearst, Welles earned a powerful enemy. The furious tycoon tried to destroy *Citizen Kane*, banning advertisements for the movie in his newspapers and even offering to buy the negatives to destroy them.

Thanks in part to Hearst's campaign against *Citizen Kane*, the film struggled to break even and faced boos at the Academy Awards. RKO Studios tossed the movie into its archive and pushed out Welles—who was only 25 years old when the movie came out. Decades later, critics around the world declared *Citizen Kane* one of the greatest movies ever made.

1946: A TEAM OF WOMEN PROGRAM ENIAC, THE FIRST ELECTRIC COMPUTER.

The first modern computer, called the ENIAC, helped the Allies win World War II. Behind the scenes, a team of six women programmed the machine, history's first electric computer. These women were the first computer programmers in history.

What did programming look like in the 1940s? The ENIAC programmers were trained mathematicians who plugged and unplugged 17,000 vacuum tubes so the machine could run equations. The programmers ran tubes between different units, calculating trajectories for the war. Instead of running complex calculations by hand, the ENIAC crunched numbers much faster.

Decades later, the women who programmed the ENIAC were recognized as some of the first computer programmers, pioneering the field of software.

1953: ROSALIND FRANKLIN HELPS DETERMINE THE STRUCTURE OF DNA.

The race to discover the structure of DNA consumed scientists around the world. In 1953, an x-ray crystallographer snapped a picture that unlocked the secret of DNA.

Rosalind Franklin, a researcher at King's College in London, used x-rays to understand the structure of proteins and molecules. In the early 1950s, one of her colleagues showed Franklin's DNA photographs to James Watson and Francis Crick, scientists at Cambridge University. The photo inspired the men to create a model of DNA as a double helix.

Watson and Crick walked away with the Nobel Prize thanks in large part to Franklin's work. Unfortunately, Franklin died of ovarian cancer at 37 without receiving recognition for her contribution.

1957: WITH THE LAUNCH OF SPUTNIK, THE SPACE AGE BEGINS.

The Soviet Union launched the first satellite into space in 1957. Named *Sputnik* and under two feet across, the satellite began the Space Age.

What did *Sputnik* do? The satellite orbited the planet several times a day, bouncing radio signals to Earth. Americans could dial in and listen to the Soviet satellite as it beeped across the sky, an orbiting reminder of their Cold War rival.

After the Soviets successfully sent a satellite into space, the U.S. fought to catch up, launching their own satellite just months later. But by then, the Soviets had already sent a dog into orbit. Just over a decade later, the Space Race put the first humans on the moon.

1963: MARTIN LUTHER KING, JR. DELIVERS HIS "I HAVE A DREAM" SPEECH.

A crowd of 250,000 marched on Washington, D.C. in 1963. Standing in front of the Lincoln Memorial, civil rights leader Martin Luther King, Jr. delivered his famous "I Have a Dream" speech.

King stayed up past midnight the night before writing his speech. And his draft never included the words "I have a dream." Instead, standing before the crowd, King spoke from his heart. "I have a dream that my four little children will one day live in a nation where they will not be judged by the color of their skin but by the content of their character."

"When this happens," King promised, all Americans could finally say "Free at last! Free at last! Thank God Almighty, we are free at last!"

1969: MAN WALKS ON THE MOON FOR THE FIRST TIME.

"That's one small step for a man, one giant leap for mankind," astronaut Neil Armstrong said as he stepped onto the Moon in 1969.

Eight years earlier, President John F. Kennedy challenged Americans to put a man on the moon before the decade ended. With months to go on the deadline, NASA sent Apollo 11 into space with three astronauts. Two—Armstrong and Buzz Aldrin—piloted the lunar module Eagle to the moon's surface.

The mission nearly ended in disaster. Armstrong had to manually steer the module over blaring computer alarms, landing with only 30 seconds of fuel left. But Apollo 11 succeeded in its mission. On Earth, 650 million people watched Armstrong walk on the moon.

1974: "LUCY," ONE OF THE OLDEST HUMAN ANCESTORS, DISCOVERED IN ETHIOPIA.

While digging in an isolated region of the Great Rift Valley, something caught anthropologist Donald Johanson's eye. The small bone, part of an elbow, belonged to an ancestor of modern humans. "As I looked up the slopes to my left I saw bits of the skull, a chunk of jaw, a couple of vertebrae," Johanson recalls.

A team of scientists recovered the skeleton and named it Lucy after the Beatles song "Lucy in the Sky with Diamonds." The find repre-sented the oldest early human ever found with one of the most complete skeletons. Decades later, scientists point to the discovery of Lucy as a monumental moment in understanding human evolution.

1977: NASA LAUNCHES THE VOYAGER 1 AND 2 SPACECRAFT.

NASA didn't just send men to the moon. It also sent mankind's knowledge out of the solar system.

In 1977, NASA launched the Voyager 1 and Voyager 2 spacecraft 16 days apart. The space probes blasted toward the solar system's outer planets, sending back reports to Earth. Realizing the spacecraft would eventually leave our solar system, NASA included two records on each probe. The records contained greetings in over 50 languages, nature sounds, and rock music. Gold engravings also provided a map back to Earth.

In 2012, Voyager 1 left the solar system, becoming the farthest man-made object from Earth. By 2025, the spacecraft will run out of energy to send messages back to Earth, but the probe will continue to travel into space.

1980: SMALLPOX IS ERADICATED

For the first time in history, humans eradicated a disease in 1980: smallpox. The deadly disease proved fatal for 30% of infected people. Smallpox killed 300 million people in the 20th century alone.

Edward Jenner developed the first smallpox vaccine in the late 18th century. Jenner used the cowpox virus to trigger an immune response. By the 20th century, smallpox vaccines used inactive versions of the smallpox virus. In 1959, the World Health Organization began its global eradication campaign, which vaccinated millions around the world.

Thanks to the smallpox vaccine, the World Health Organization officially announced the eradication of smallpox in 1980.

1991: THE FIRST WEBSITE IS PUT ONLINE AND MADE AVAILABLE TO THE PUBLIC.

Home computers and the internet changed the world. In 1991, the first website went live, marking a major step in the new digital age.

What did the first website look like? CERN, Europe's organization for nuclear research, posted the first website. In its early years, scientists saw the potential for the internet to connect researchers around the world. CERN could instantly share information with institutes across the globe using the internet.

As for what the webpage said, it contained instructions on the World Wide Web project. The text explained how to create websites, how to use hypertext, and creating web servers. As other sites went online, the very first webpage included links to everything on the web.

2001: THE HUMAN GENOME PROJECT PUBLISHES THE COMPLETE HUMAN GENOME.

The Human Genome Project began mapping the complete human genetic code in 1990. By 2001, the Human Genome Project had a genetic blueprint for mankind.

The project promised unrestricted access to the genetic code, publishing sequence information within 24 hours of creating it. Over 200 labs in the U.S. contributed to the project, along with labs in 18 other countries. The work of the Human Genome Project unlocked new possibilities for genetic medicine. Sequencing human genes shed new light on the causes of cancer, genetic disorders, and other conditions.

Creating the first draft of a human genome cost $300 million. Two decades later, we can sequence an entire human genome for $100.

2006: SCIENTISTS RECLASSIFY PLUTO AS A DWARF PLANET.

Generations grew up learning about the nine planets in the solar system—until the International Astronomical Union announced that Pluto was not a planet in 2006.

Planets must orbit a star, take a spherical shape, and clear its neighboring region of objects. While Pluto met the first two criteria, it failed on number three. Pluto simply isn't large enough for its gravitational force to sweep away space debris. Thus Pluto became a dwarf planet, bringing the number of planets in the solar system down to eight.

In the distant Kuiper belt, Pluto isn't alone. It shares outer space with four other dwarf planets, known as plutinos: Ceres, Makemake, Haumea, and Eris.

2019: SCIENTISTS CAPTURE THE IMAGE OF A BLACK HOLE.

As the Voyager spacecraft left our solar system, scientists took the first picture of a black hole.

Black holes pull in light, consuming nearby stars and planets. Their very nature—and their distance from Earth—made it almost impossible to photograph a black hole. How could scientists take a picture of something perfectly black in space?

Katie Bouman, a 29-year-old computer scientist at MIT, created the computer program that made the photograph possible. Researchers used linked radio dishes from the South Pole to the U.S. to turn the Earth into a virtual telescope. Backlit by gasses at its event horizon, the black hole appears in silhouette in the photograph.

Just how hard was it to photograph the black hole? It was the equivalent of taking a picture of an orange on the surface of the moon.

CONCLUSION

The scope of history is humbling. We're closer to the time when Cleopatra lived than Cleopatra was to the building of the pyramids.

By stepping back and looking at history more broadly, it's easier to see some patterns. Throughout history, people have worked to understand the world around them. Ancient Chinese astronomers cataloged comets while ancient Greeks measured the size of the Earth.

And each step in human knowledge builds on previous steps—even when they're incorrect. Aristotle's theory of gravity relied on the nature of the elements. Anything made of earth wanted to move to the center of the universe, so a rock fell if you dropped it.

Centuries later, Copernicus claimed the Earth wasn't at the center of the universe. For decades, scientists searched for a new way to explain gravity. But it wasn't until Newton, 150 years after Copernicus, that scientists agreed on a new theory of gravity. Without Aristotle's theory, Newton might not have developed his own.

"If I have seen farther than others," Newton said, "it is because I have stood on the shoulders of giants."

We also see the ways rulers and empires rise and fall. Accidents of birth and death cast a long shadow in history. Louis XIV became King of France at just four years old after his father's death, and he outlived his own sons. The death of Alexander the Great at only 32 years old ended the ruler's campaign to build a massive empire. And when Henry VIII's wives didn't produce a male heir, it fractured the relationship between England and the Catholic Church.

The choices made in one part of the world shape what happens in distant lands. Japan chose to close its borders to Western influence. European powers created colonies and exploited their
resources. Ming China rejected anything foreign after Mongol rule.

In the earliest days of history, writing took centuries to spread from one part of the world to another. By the classical period, travelers crossed cultural boundaries and shared stories. In ancient Rome, worshippers prayed to the Egyptian goddess Isis. In ancient China, merchants trod the Silk Road to carry luxurious fabric and jade to the Near East.

The medieval world grew increasingly linked, as sailors crossed the Indian Ocean to trade goods while the Mongols built history's largest land empire. Thanks to the Mongols, Persian artists began incorporating Chinese dragons into their motifs and Europeans like Marco Polo traveled the Silk Road for the first time.

During the Age of Discovery, Chinese treasure ships sailed to Africa and European galleons crossed the Atlantic. But discovery didn't only mean exploration—it meant learning more about the world itself. Networks of scientists from the Americas to Eurasia compared information and over-turned classical theories. New foods circled the globe as the Old and New World compared culinary notes.

By the modern era, technology connected the world. A message that would have taken weeks to cross the Atlantic suddenly took seconds thanks to the first transatlantic telegraph cable. Cars, radio, planes, and television made the world feel even smaller.

The 21st century will present new challenges for the world. But by looking back at history, we can see how far we've come—and how much we've overcome. Without understanding the past, we can't meet the future.

TO LEARN MORE . . .

One Day at a Time explores 365 snapshots from history. If these moments from the past leave you wanting more—great! There are always more puzzles, mysteries, and stories in history.

Here's the good news: you don't have to earn a graduate degree in history to learn more about the past. You can start with a simple internet search. Wikipedia is a great starting point to learn more. Even history professors visit Wikipedia, and its timelines helped inspire this project.

Then, check out online resources like Ancient History Encyclopedia, Atlas Obscura, and History Extra, the website for the BBC History Magazine. These sites, and others like All That's Interesting, Historic-UK, and History.com, include articles on every topic imaginable. If you prefer podcasts, check out Stuff You Missed in History Class.

If you'd like to jump into primary sources, EuroDocs includes online sources for European history, while the Internet History Sourcebooks Project collects public domain historical texts from every time period. The Google Cultural Institute includes artworks from around the world.

Above all else, stay curious. Follow your curiosity and see where you end up. When you learn something from the past, share it with someone in your life. And draw on the past to meet challenges in the future.

ABOUT THE AUTHOR

Bruce Wilson, Jr., is passionate about many things, including travel, spending time with family and friends, and college football—especially his alma mater the University of Georgia where he graduated with a degree in English.

Even though his profession has been in the commercial real estate space, Bruce is most passionate about people and their journey through time. This book reflects that passion.

One Day at a Time captures the essence of the lives of prominent people across time: their explorations, inventions, and their successes in spite of the inevitable difficulties we all share as we try to overcome challenges and make a difference for good.

Bruce hopes readers walk away from *One Day at a Time* fascinated by our shared history. We all need to remember where we came from and how we got here to motivate ourselves and stimulate our minds. We can also learn about "what works" and "what doesn't work" from the past.

IMAGE CREDITS

A Sumerian bill of contract to sell a house, c. 2600 BCE
    Louvre Museum/Public Domain

The Egyptian pyramids, photographed in 2017
    Muhamed Ayman/CC-BY-SA-4.0

The Parthenon, photographed in 2005
    Thermos/CC-BY-SA-2.5

Cleopatra, by John William Waterhouse (1887)
    Ángel M. Felicísimo/CC-BY-2.0

Roman aqueducts in 2015
    Don Zaucker/CC-BY-SA-4.0

Nazca lines in Peru
    NASA/Public Domain

Venus de Milo, currently at the Louvre Museum
    Mattgirling/CC-BY-3.0

A copy of the 1602 world map by Matteo Ricci
Tohoku University Library/Public Domain

Self-Portrait as the Allegory of Painting by Artemisia Gentileschi (1638)
Royal Collection/Public Domain

Benjamin Franklin's political cartoon, Join or Die, from 1754
Library of Congress/Public Domain

A hot air balloon lifting off in Paris in 1783, by Claude-Louis Desrais
Bibliothèque nationale de France/Public Domain

The Frost Fair of the river Thames 1684, by Rita Greer
Public Domain

John Snow's cholera map showing the Broad Street Pump, 1854
Public Domain

The Eiffel Tower during the Paris Exhibition of 1889
Library of Congress/Public Domain

Buzz Aldrin walking on the moon in 1969
NASA/Public Domain